Student Activity W

Joan Kelly-Plate
Career Educator
Lake Suzy, Florida

Ruth Volz-Patton
Career Consultant
Springfield, Illinois

Glencoe

New York, New York   Columbus, Ohio   Chicago, Illinois

Glencoe

The *McGraw-Hill* Companies

Send all inquiries to:
Glencoe/McGraw-Hill
21600 Oxnard Street, Suite 500
Woodland Hills, CA 91367

ISBN-13: 978-0-07-873692-6 (Student Edition)
ISBN-10: 0-07-873692-7   (Student Edition)
ISBN-13: 978-0-07-873693-3 (Teacher Annotated Edition)
ISBN-10: 0-07-873693-5   (Teacher Annotated Edition)

10 11 12 13 DOH 18 17 16 15

Table of Contents

File in your Career Resource File.

CHAPTER 1 Self Awareness

ACTIVITY 1   *Check Out Your Interests*
for use with Lesson 1.1

Your Goal: Identify your own interests that could lead to the choice of a future career.

What to Do: Read the directions for each section below. Check the responses that tell your true feelings.

People—Information—Technology

Organize Your Information: Check each item according to how much you enjoy doing it—*Often/Fairly Often, Sometimes,* or *Never/Hardly Ever.*

Category		Often/ Fairly Often	Sometimes	Never/ Hardly Ever
People	Enjoy being with people	☐	☐	☐
	Get along well with people	☐	☐	☐
	Like to talk with people	☐	☐	☐
	Want to help people	☐	☐	☐
Information	Read books/magazines for information	☐	☐	☐
	Like to learn about new things	☐	☐	☐
	Take pride in knowing facts	☐	☐	☐
	Seek out information	☐	☐	☐
Technology	Like to work with my hands	☐	☐	☐
	Enjoy repairing things	☐	☐	☐
	Want to know how things work	☐	☐	☐
	Good at figuring out how to put things together	☐	☐	☐

Hobbies

Organize Your Information: What hobbies do you enjoy? Read the following list of hobby categories. Put a check next to the type of hobby you have or would like to have. Then write a description of your specific hobby and tell why you enjoy it. For example, if you check "Collecting," tell what you collect—coins, stamps, etc.—and why you enjoy this hobby.

I Enjoy   **Type of Hobby, What I Do, and What I Enjoy Most**

☐ Collecting: _____

☐ Sports: _____

Continued on next page

☐ Music: _____

☐ Reading: _____

☐ Animals/pets: _____

☐ Sewing/fashion: _____

☐ Art/drawing: _____

☐ Cooking: _____

☐ Other: _____

Activities

Organize Your Information: What activities do you participate in outside of the classroom? What role do you play in each activity? Are you an officer or a member? In the exercise below, check the activities you are involved in. Then describe your involvement.

I Enjoy | **Type of Activity and What I Do**

☐ School clubs (list and describe each one): _____

☐ Student council/ government: _____

☐ Band/orchestra/ drama/dance/singing: _____

☐ Cheerleader/ pep squad: _____

☐ School newspaper: _____

☐ Sports (list each one): _____

Television Programs

Organize Your Information: Put a check next to the type of television programs you usually watch each week. Then list your two or three favorite shows in each checked category.

I Enjoy | **Type of Shows I Watch and My Favorite Programs**

☐ Sports shows: _____

☐ Adventure/mystery: _____

☐ Drama/ human interest: _____

☐ Science fiction: _____

☐ Situation comedies: _____

☐ Cartoons: _____

☐ Game shows: _____

☐ Music shows: _____

☐ News: _____

☐ Soap operas: _____

☐ Science: _____

☐ Other: _____

School Subjects

Organize Your Information: Which school subjects are your favorites? Put a check next to the subjects you do well in and like. Then describe what you like most about these subjects.

I Enjoy   **What I Enjoy Most**

☐ English: _____

☐ Sciences: _____

☐ Math: _____

☐ Foreign languages: _____

☐ Social studies/
history/geography: _____

☐ Computer science: _____

☐ Physical education/
sports: _____

☐ Home economics
(for example, cooking): _____

☐ Industrial arts
(for example,
auto mechanics): _____

☐ Music/art/drama: _____

☐ Other: _____

Books and Magazines

Organize Your Information: When you read books or magazines, what type do you read? Check the types you like to read. Then list your favorites.

I Enjoy   **My Favorite Books or Magazines**

☐ Sports: _____

☐ Mechanics/cars: _____

Continued on next page

☐ People/celebrities: _____

☐ Science: _____

☐ Humor: _____

☐ Fashion: _____

☐ Space: _____

☐ Animals: _____

☐ Computers: _____

☐ Current news events: _____

☐ History: _____

☐ Other: _____

Summarize Your Interests

Make a Decision: Look back at your answers in each category. Pick your top three choices in each section and write them in the spaces below.

People/Information/Technology	1._____	2._____	3._____
Hobbies	1._____	2._____	3._____
Activities	1._____	2._____	3._____
Television Programs	1._____	2._____	3._____
School Subjects	1._____	2._____	3._____
Books/Magazines	1._____	2._____	3._____

Critical Thinking

1. Look at the interests listed above in "Summarize Your Interests." List the three things you like to do the most.

_____   _____   _____

2. What types of jobs do you think might include these interests? For example, if you like to fix things, you might like a career in computer repair or electronics.

_____

_____

File in your Career Resource File.

CHAPTER **1** Self Awareness

ACTIVITY 2   *Know Your Work Values*
for use with Lesson 1.1

Your Goal: Identify your own values that could help you in choosing a future career.

What to Do: Below are some values related to work. Some of these values will be more important to you than others. Use the rating scale below to show how important each value is to you. Use your decision-making skills to put a check in one of these columns: *Very Important, Somewhat Important,* or *Not Important.*

Values	Very Important	Somewhat Important	Not Important
Being paid a lot	☐	☐	☐
Being independent	☐	☐	☐
Having a regular routine	☐	☐	☐
Helping others	☐	☐	☐
Making changes in society	☐	☐	☐
Feeling important or being recognized	☐	☐	☐
Being creative	☐	☐	☐
Having a variety of things to do	☐	☐	☐
Leading others	☐	☐	☐
Not having to worry about losing my job	☐	☐	☐

Critical Thinking

1. Look back at the values you rated as "very important." List five of these in order of importance to you. Begin with the most important, the next most important, and so on. This process is called prioritizing.

What I value the most:

_____

_____

_____

_____

_____

Continued on next page

2. Look at the values you rated as "not important." List five of these in order of their lack of importance to you. Begin with the least important of all.

What I value the least:

_____

_____

_____

_____

_____

3. What do your values tell you about the type of work you would be happy doing? For example, if you value having a regular routine, what type of work would give you a regular routine?

_____

_____

_____

_____

_____

_____

_____

_____

4. Do your work values show you can choose more than one type of work? Name three types of work you could do.

_____

_____

_____

_____

_____

_____

_____

_____

CHAPTER 1 Self Awareness

File in your Career Resource File.

ACTIVITY 3   *Add Up Your Skills and Aptitudes*

for use with Lesson 1.2

Your Goal: Identify your own skills and aptitudes that may help you in your career choice.

What to Do: Look at the list of skills and aptitudes listed below. Rate yourself on each by checking one of these responses: *strong, fair, not strong.*

Skills/Aptitudes	Strong	Fair	Not Strong
Working with special tools	☐	☐	☐
Operating machines	☐	☐	☐
Drawing	☐	☐	☐
Speaking in front of an audience	☐	☐	☐
Writing	☐	☐	☐
Working with numbers	☐	☐	☐
Typing rapidly	☐	☐	☐
Solving problems	☐	☐	☐
Organizing schedules	☐	☐	☐
Entertaining others	☐	☐	☐

Critical Thinking

1. Look back over your responses. Which are your strongest skills and aptitudes? Write your five top skills/aptitudes in the spaces below. If you have other skills/aptitudes that were not listed above, include those in your list.

   My five top skills or aptitudes:

   _____

   _____

   _____

   _____

   _____

   _____

   _____

   _____

Continued on next page

Chapter 1 • Exploring Careers   7

2. How would you describe your skills/aptitudes? Write a sentence to describe each strength.

_____

_____

_____

_____

_____

_____

_____

3. Which of your skills are transferable skills? Write a sentence describing why these skills are transferable.

_____

_____

_____

_____

_____

_____

_____

4. How do you think your skills and aptitudes will influence your choice of a career?

_____

_____

_____

_____

_____

_____

_____

_____

File in
your Career
Resource File.

CHAPTER **1** Self Awareness

ACTIVITY 4   *Profile Your Personality*
for use with Lesson 1.3

Your Goal: Learn more about your own personality traits to help you in your career choice.

What to Do: Read the words below that describe people. Circle the words that describe you the most. After you do this, answer the questions that follow.

Personality Characteristics

outgoing	fun-loving	calm
friendly	quiet	brave
playful	energetic	helpful
serious	agreeable	imaginative
caring	loyal	patient
confident	cheerful	thoughtful
dependable	generous	intelligent
shy	lively	respectful
kind	organized	happy
strong	rebellious	unpredictable
trustworthy	responsible	worried
warm	stubborn	sensitive
immature	fair	sociable

Continued on next page

Critical Thinking

1. From the list above, write down the five personality characteristics that best describe you.

_____

_____

_____

_____

_____

_____

2. Because you have these characteristics, what kind of work do you think best suits you? For example, if you are outgoing and friendly, you might work as a salesperson.

List five possible jobs that might fit with your personality.

_____

_____

_____

_____

_____

_____

_____

_____

_____

_____

_____

_____

_____

_____

CHAPTER 1 Self Awareness

File in your Career Resource File.

ACTIVITY 5   *Discover How You Learn Best*

for use with Lesson 1.3

Your Goal: Find out how you learn in order to look for a career that uses your strongest learning style.

What to Do: Below is a list of eight different ways that people learn things. Read the descriptions of the learning styles and decide which one fits you the best. Then list your three top ways of learning. Have some fun by trying to match the learning style in one column with a job title in the other column.

Learning Styles

1. *Verbal/Linguistic:* You like to read, write, and listen to others talk. You learn best through listening, speaking, and writing.

2. *Logical/Mathematical:* You like to do experiments and work with numbers. You learn best by making categories, solving arithmetic problems, and working with patterns.

3. *Bodily/Kinesthetic:* You like to dance and participate in athletic activities. You learn best through body movement.

4. *Visual/Spatial:* You like to draw, build, design, and create things. You learn best through pictures, videos, and images.

5. *Musical/Rhythmic:* You like to sing, hum, play an instrument, and listen to music. You learn best through rhythm and melody.

6. *Interpersonal:* You like having many friends, talking to people, and joining groups. You learn best through talking, comparing, and cooperating with other people.

7. *Intrapersonal:* You like to work alone and pursue interests at your own pace. You learn best by yourself.

8. *Naturalistic:* You like to work with plants and animals. You learn best in a natural environment.

My three top ways of learning:

_____

_____

_____

Continued on next page

     Chapter 1 • Exploring Careers   **11**

Match the learning style with a job title by putting the letter of the job title in the space next to the learning style.

_____	Interpersonal	A. Cartoonist
_____	Logical/Mathematical	B. President of a company
_____	Musical/Rhythmic	C. Ballet dancer
_____	Intrapersonal	D. Novel writer
_____	Visual/Spatial	E. Accountant
_____	Bodily/Kinesthetic	F. Counselor
_____	Verbal/Linguistic	G. Guitar player
_____	Naturalistic	H. Park ranger

Critical Thinking

1. Think about how you learn in school. Do you feel more comfortable in your math class or in your physical education class? You probably learn the best in the class in which you feel the most comfortable. List below the three classes in which you are the happiest.

My three favorite classes:

_____

_____

_____

_____

2. Now try to think of jobs that would be similar to those three classes. For example, you might like your art class the best. A good job might be a graphic designer.

Three jobs that might be similar to my favorite classes:

_____

_____

_____

_____

_____

CHAPTER 2 Thinking About Work

ACTIVITY 1 *What Kinds of Jobs Are There?*

for use with Lesson 2.1

Your Goal: Explore the variety of jobs to be found in a business.

What to Do: Write as many jobs as you can think of under each type of business listed below. After you complete your lists, answer the Critical Thinking questions.

Jobs Associated With

A Large Hotel	A Movie Production Company	An Airline
_____	_____	_____
_____	_____	_____
_____	_____	_____
_____	_____	_____

Critical Thinking

Pick one job from each of the three columns above. Answer the following questions about each one.

1. What training do you think people need for each job? Write a brief description of the kind of education and training you think you would need to do each job successfully.

Job	Training Needed
_____	_____
_____	_____
_____	_____
_____	_____

Continued on next page

2. How would you describe the work setting for each of the three jobs?

Job   **Work Setting**

_____   _____

_____   _____

_____   _____

3. What type of work schedules do the people working in each of the three jobs probably have?

Job   **Work Schedules**

_____   _____

_____   _____

_____   _____

4. For each type of work—a large hotel, a movie production company, and an airline—pick the one job listed that you would most like to have. Explain why you would like this job. If there are no jobs that you would like, choose the three jobs you would least like to have. Explain why.

Job   **Why I Would/Wouldn't Like This Job**

_____   _____

                                    _____

                                    _____

_____   _____

                                    _____

                                    _____

_____   _____

                                    _____

                                    _____

                                    _____

                                    _____

File in your Career Resource File.

CHAPTER 2 Thinking About Work

ACTIVITY 2   *Why Will You Work?*

for use with Lesson 2.1

Your Goal: Explore your own personal reasons for working.

What to Do: Complete each of the statements. This will give you a clearer picture of what's important to you.

1. People work for money.
   I will work to earn money for the following reasons (an example is *I want to buy a car*):

   _____

   _____

   _____

   _____

2. People work for recognition.
   I want my work to give me recognition for the following things (an example is *I want to be recognized for my singing ability*):

   _____

   _____

   _____

3. People work to feel good about themselves.
   At work I want to feel good about the following things (an example is *I want to feel good about knowing how to treat the customers properly*):

   _____

   _____

   _____

   _____

Continued on next page

Chapter 2 • Exploring Careers   15

4. People work to be useful.

At my work, I want to be useful by doing the following things (an example is *I want to be useful by helping others*):

_____

_____

_____

5. People work to be with others.

At work I want to be with other people for the following reasons (an example is *I want to be with others so that I can gain new friends and share ideas*):

_____

_____

_____

_____

6. Can you think of any other reasons you will have for wanting to work? List those reasons.

_____

_____

_____

Critical Thinking

1. What is your most important reason for working? Explain why it is the most important.

_____

_____

_____

_____

2. What is your least important reason for working? Explain why it is the least important.

_____

_____

_____

_____

File in your Career Resource File.

CHAPTER 2 Thinking About Work

ACTIVITY 3   *A Job or a Career?*

for use with Lesson 2.1

Your Goal: Discover what jobs you can do to help you achieve your career goal.

What to Do: Pick a career that might interest you. It might be a career working with computers, working with animals, working in the restaurant business, or in some other area.

   List all of the jobs you can think of that you might have in this career field. After you list the jobs, answer the Critical Thinking questions.

The career field that interests me is:

_____

Jobs that I can hold in this career field include:

_____

_____

Critical Thinking

1. Which of these jobs can I do while I am still in school?

   _____

   _____

2. How would I benefit from having one of these jobs while I am still in school?

   _____

   _____

3. What school classes could I take to prepare myself for my career field?

   _____

   _____

CHAPTER 2 Thinking About Work

File in your Career Resource File.

| ACTIVITY 4 | *What Are Your Goals?* |

for use with Lesson 2.1

Your Goal: Predict what you will be doing for the next 5, 10, 15, and 20 years.

What to Do: In each of the blocks below, write your dream for that 5-year period. Tell what you want to accomplish in your personal life, such as starting a family, travel, or home ownership. Then tell what you expect to accomplish in your career, such as attending college or getting a raise in pay.

Dates	What I Want to Accomplish in My Personal Life	What I Want to Accomplish in My Career
5 years from now I will be _____ years old.		
10 years from now I will be _____ years old.		
15 years from now I will be _____ years old.		
20 years from now I will be _____ years old.		

CHAPTER 2 Thinking About Work

ACTIVITY 5   *Changes in the Work World*
for use with Lesson 2.2

Your Goal: Analyze the way current events are changing the world in which you will be working.

What to Do: Read a newspaper or watch a news program on TV. Which events in the news do you think will affect work and jobs? In the space below summarize two of the news stories. Select the stories that describe events you think will have the greatest effect on the work that people do. Then answer the Critical Thinking questions.

News Story 1

Source: _____ Title of News Story: _____

Summary of what the news story said:

_____

_____

_____

_____

_____

_____

News Story 2

Source: _____ Title of News Story: _____

Summary:

_____

_____

_____

_____

_____

_____

Continued on next page

Chapter 2 • Exploring Careers   19

Critical Thinking

1. How will the events in this news story affect work and jobs? For example, will the events in this news story change the kinds of training necessary?

News Story 1:

_____

_____

_____

_____

News Story 2:

_____

_____

_____

_____

2. Do workers need to prepare for the changes described in question 1? What could they do?

News Story 1:

_____

_____

_____

_____

News Story 2:

_____

_____

_____

_____

CHAPTER 2 Thinking About Work

File in your Career Resource File.

| ACTIVITY 6 | *Taking Charge of Your Working Life* |

for use with Lesson 2.2

Your Goal: Identify the things you can and cannot control in the world of work.

What to Do: Read the list of events and activities below. Write the events and activities you can control under the *I Can Control* column. Write the events and activities you cannot control under the *I Cannot Control* column. For this exercise, pretend that you are working for a large company.

An example of something you can control is getting an education. An example of something you cannot control is whether the company hires more workers.

Events and Activities in the World of Work

Getting an education
Getting along with fellow workers
Prices of goods and services rising
Getting information about careers
Employees being laid off from work
Doing a job well
Dressing properly for the job
Global economy and technology changes
More workers being hired

Workers taking a pay cut
Getting special training
Getting part-time job experience
Businesses moving out of town or out of
  the country
Getting to work on time
Rules of the company changing
More workers telecommuting (working
  at home)

I Can Control	I Cannot Control
_____	_____
_____	_____
_____	_____
_____	_____
_____	_____
_____	_____
_____	_____
_____	_____

Continued on next page

Critical Thinking

1. Summarize in two or three sentences one type of event or activity in the world of work that you *can* control and explain how you can control it.

_____

_____

_____

_____

_____

2. Summarize in two or three sentences one type of event or activity in the world of work that you *cannot* control and explain why you cannot control it.

_____

_____

_____

_____

_____

3. From the list on the previous page, choose three things that you could do to give yourself more control over your life at work and to prepare yourself for changes in the world of work.

_____

_____

_____

_____

_____

_____

_____

CHAPTER 2 Thinking About Work

ACTIVITY 7   *Preparing for Change*

for use with Lesson 2.2

Your Goal: Look at the way you handle change in your life.

What to Do: Answer questions 1 through 4 by checking *Usually*,
Sometimes, or *Rarely*. Then give an example to illustrate your answer.

You and Change

1. Do you adjust to changes easily?

   ☐ Usually   ☐ Sometimes   ☐ Rarely

   Explain: _____

   _____

   _____

2. Do changes occur for the best?

   ☐ Usually   ☐ Sometimes   ☐ Rarely

   Explain: _____

   _____

   _____

3. Do you enjoy learning new tasks, skills, and information?

   ☐ Usually   ☐ Sometimes   ☐ Rarely

   Explain: _____

   _____

   _____

4. Would you rather that things remain the same?

   ☐ Usually   ☐ Sometimes   ☐ Rarely

   Explain: _____

   _____

   _____

Continued on next page

Critical Thinking

1. Give an example of a change you have had to make recently. For example, you might have changed your school schedule or changed your general routine at home. Describe how you handled that change.

_____

_____

_____

_____

2. In general, describe the way you accept and prepare for change.

_____

_____

_____

_____

3. Are you satisfied with the way you handle change? ☐ Yes   ☐ No

   Explain: _____

_____

_____

_____

_____

4. If you checked _No_ in number 3, answer this question: What can you do now to help yourself adjust more easily to changes in the future?

_____

_____

_____

_____

CHAPTER 2 Thinking About Work

Employment Trends
for use with Lesson 2.2

Your Goal: Examine an employment trend.

What to Do: Read an article in a magazine, newspaper, or on the Internet about an employment trend. If you have difficulty locating an article, go to the reference section of your library. Keywords are *employment*, *manufacturing*, *unemployment*, and *technology*.

Employment Trend Article

Source: _____ Title of Article: _____

Summary of article:

_____

_____

_____

_____

_____

_____

_____

1. What do you believe is causing this employment trend?

_____

_____

_____

2. Will this employment trend affect you? How?

_____

_____

_____

Continued on next page

3. Will this employment trend affect others? How?

_____

_____

_____

4. What effect will this employment trend have on the goods and services you use?

_____

_____

_____

5. Will this employment trend be a short-term or long-term trend? Why?

_____

_____

_____

Critical Thinking

1. How can education help you or others prepare for this employment trend?

_____

_____

_____

_____

_____

2. What other things can you do to prepare for this trend?

_____

_____

_____

_____

_____

_____

Name	Class	Teacher

Date Assigned	Date Completed

File in your Career Resource File.

CHAPTER 3 Researching Careers

for use with Lesson 3.1

Your Goal: Choose a career cluster that interests you.

What to Do: Select one career cluster that interests you most right now. Then answer the questions that follow.

Career Clusters:

Agriculture, Food, and Natural Resources
Architecture and Construction
Arts, Audio/Video Technology,
  and Communications
Business, Management, and Administration
Education and Training
Finance
Government and Public Administration
Health Science

Hospitality and Tourism
Human Services
Information Technology
Law, Public Safety, and Security
Manufacturing
Marketing, Sales, and Service
Science, Technology, Engineering,
  and Mathematics
Transportation, Distribution, and Logistics

Critical Thinking

1. Name the career cluster that interests you most right now. Give three reasons why. For example, the Finance career cluster might tie in with your aptitude in math.

_____

_____

_____

_____

_____

2. What specific occupations for that career cluster interest you? List them below. Refer to your text for suggestions.

_____

_____

_____

_____

Continued on next page

3. What training or education do you think will be needed for the occupations you have listed?

_____

_____

_____

_____

_____

4. List your skills and aptitudes below. Use the list that you made in a previous activity or create a new list. Now compare your skills and aptitudes with the cluster you've selected. Do your skills match the occupations you've listed? Explain how they do or do not match the occupations.

_____

_____

_____

_____

_____

5. What conditions of work or what surroundings do you especially like? What do you think you wouldn't like? For example, you might like to be outdoors most of your work day. You might not want to be in an office all day.

Like	**Dislike**
_____	_____
_____	_____
_____	_____
_____	_____
_____	_____
_____	_____

CHAPTER 3 Researching Careers

File in
your Career
Resource File.

ACTIVITY 2   *Career Interest Areas*

for use with Lesson 3.1

Your Goal: Rate yourself in six career interest areas to help you in choosing a career.

What to Do: Look over the career interest areas below and rate yourself from 1 to 5 for each area. If you circle 1, that means you do not fit that description. If you circle 5, that means you strongly fit that description. Then answer the Critical Thinking questions that follow.

Career Interest Area	My Interests	Rating				
Creator	Creative thinker. Independent, artistic. I like to use materials or machines.	1	2	3	4	5
Investigator	Logical thinker. I like experiments, research, science, math, and history.	1	2	3	4	5
Influencer	A leader, good at convincing others. I am a risk-taker.	1	2	3	4	5
Organizer	I like to be neat, organized, and follow rules. I work well as part of a team.	1	2	3	4	5
Doer	I'm always busy and full of energy. I like to use tools and machinery. I love to be outdoors.	1	2	3	4	5
Helper	I am friendly, fun, patient. I am always ready to help. I'm a good communicator.	1	2	3	4	5

Continued on next page

Critical Thinking

1. Which description from the list of career interest areas fits you the best?

_____

_____

_____

2. Give two examples of what you do that makes that description fit you.

_____

_____

_____

_____

3. Which description fits you the least?

_____

_____

4. What career clusters match the descriptions that fit you? List as many as you can. Then give the reason those career clusters match your career interest areas.

_____

_____

_____

_____

_____

_____

_____

_____

_____

_____

_____

_____

_____

_____

CHAPTER 3 Researching Careers

File in your Career Resource File.

ACTIVITY 3 *Checking Out Sources of Information*

for use with Lesson 3.2

Your Goal: Research career information in three sources.

What to Do: Check out three sources of information about careers. The source can be printed or online. You may find the following in your library or guidance office at school:

- *Dictionary of Occupational Titles*
- *Occupational Outlook Handbook*
- *Guide for Occupational Exploration*
- Computerized Guidance Program
- Other publications, such as books, magazines, and audiovisuals.

Researching information: Examine each publication or resource. Look up information on a career you are interested in. Then complete the following information.

Title of Source #1: _____

1. Career I'm researching _____

2. What did you learn from this source?

   Training and education needed _____

   _____

   _____

   Conditions of work _____

   _____

   _____

   Pay or salary _____

   _____

3. What was most helpful about this source? Why was it helpful? _____

   _____

   _____

Continued on next page

Title of Source #2: _____

1. Career I'm researching _____

2. What did you learn from this source?

   Training and education needed _____

   _____

   _____

   Conditions of work _____

   _____

   _____

   Pay or salary _____

   _____

3. What was most helpful about this source? Why was it helpful? _____

   _____

   _____

Title of Source #3: _____

1. Career I'm researching _____

2. What did you learn from this source?

   Training and education needed _____

   _____

   _____

   Conditions of work _____

   _____

   _____

   Pay or salary _____

   _____

3. What was most helpful about this source? Why was it helpful? _____

   _____

   _____

CHAPTER **3** Researching Careers

File in your Career Resource File.

ACTIVITY 4 *Talking to Others About Their Work*

for use with Lesson 3.2

Your Goal: Get information about work by interviewing workers in your community.

What to Do: Interview two people about their work. If possible, talk to someone working in a career that interests you. Take notes as you ask the following questions. Then think about what you learned and answer the Critical Thinking questions.

Interview #1: Job Title _____

1. What do you do at work? _____

   _____

2. What are your work surroundings like? _____

3. Is your routine the same every day or is it different? _____

4. Do you work alone or with other people? Do you like the amount of contact you have

   with people? _____

5. What kind of education or training do you need for this job? _____

6. What kind of personality characteristics are helpful in your work? _____

7. What do you like most about your work? _____

8. What do you like least about your work? _____

9. What are the chances for advancement in your work? _____

10. Where can a person be located with a job such as yours? _____

11. What is your work schedule? _____

Interview #2: Job Title _____

1. What do you do at work? _____

   _____

2. What are your work surroundings like? _____

Continued on next page

3. Is your routine the same every day or is it different? _____

4. Do you work alone or with other people? Do you like the amount of contact you have with people? _____

5. What kind of education or training do you need for this job? _____

6. What kind of personality characteristics are helpful in your work? _____

7. What do you like most about your work? _____

8. What do you like least about your work? _____

9. What are the chances for advancement in your work? _____

10. Where can a person be located with a job such as yours? _____

11. What is your work schedule? _____

Critical Thinking

1. What did you learn about the career? _____

_____

2. What did you like the most about the two jobs? Why?

   Job from Interview #1: _____

   Job from Interview #2: _____

   _____

3. What did you like the least about the two jobs? Why?

   Job from Interview #1: _____

   _____

   Job from Interview #2: _____

   _____

4. Would you consider working in either of the two jobs? Why or why not?

   Job from Interview #1: _____

   _____

   Job from Interview #2: _____

   _____

File in
your Career
Resource File.

CHAPTER 3 Researching Careers

ACTIVITY 5   *Careers in Your Community*

for use with Lesson 3.2

Your Goal: Find out whether your community offers career opportunities for you.

What to Do: Evaluate the career possibilities in your community by doing your own research.

Types of Employment

1. Research the types of employment in your community.
   - Talk to people about the types of employment where you live.
   - Read the newspaper to see if there are articles about employment in your community.
   - Check with the Chamber of Commerce, the library, or online for material about local industry or business and employment information.

Opportunities

2. List below the employment areas you discovered in your research about your community. Put a check mark in either the column marked *many good opportunities* or *few opportunities* for each employment area in your community.

Types of Employment	Many Good Opportunities	Few Opportunities
_____	☐	☐
_____	☐	☐
_____	☐	☐
_____	☐	☐
_____	☐	☐
_____	☐	☐
_____	☐	☐
_____	☐	☐
_____	☐	☐
_____	☐	☐

Continued on next page

     Chapter 3 • Exploring Careers   **35**

Jobs Connected with Types of Employment

3. Select one of the employment types you listed. List all of the jobs connected with that type of employment. You may know about some of these jobs. If not, contact the business to find out about the different jobs.

_____

_____

_____

_____

_____

Critical Thinking

1. Do the types of employment in your community match your career interests? If yes, how do they match? If no, where would you need to go to find a community to match your career interests?

_____

_____

_____

_____

_____

2. What does the answer above mean to you and your career? Will you be able to find a job in your community or will you have to move to another community?

_____

_____

_____

_____

_____

_____

_____

_____

CHAPTER 3 Researching Careers

File in your Career Resource File.

ACTIVITY 6 *Researching Your Career*

for use with Lesson 3.2

Your Goal: Analyze two careers to see if they fit your own personal needs.

What to Do: Answer the questions in this activity. Use the information about your interests, skills, work values, personality characteristics, and your reasons for working that you organized in Chapters 1 and 2.

You will also need resources such as the *Occupational Outlook Handbook,* the *Guide for Occupational Exploration,* or online career resources.

Organize Your Information

The first career that interests me is _____

1. Skills/Aptitudes

   What skills are needed? _____

   What skills do I have? _____

2. Education and training

   What education and training are needed? _____

   _____

   What education and training will I have when I complete high school? _____

   _____

   What education and training will I be able to obtain after high school? _____

   _____

3. Work Setting

   What is the work setting like? _____

   What type of work setting do I prefer? _____

Continued on next page

4. Hours

What hours are required? _____

What hours do I prefer? _____

5. Duties and Responsibilities

What are the responsibilities? _____

_____

What responsibilities do I prefer? _____

_____

6. Personality characteristics

What type of personality would be successful? _____

What type of personality do I have? _____

7. Location

Where is the work located? _____

What location do I prefer? _____

8. Advancement

What are the advancement opportunities? _____

What advancement do I look forward to? _____

9. Job outlook

What is the job outlook? _____

Will there be jobs available for me? _____

10. What is the expected pay in this career? _____

Will this pay match what I would like to receive? _____

Organize Your Information

The second career that interests me is _____

1. Skills/Aptitudes

What skills are needed? _____

What skills do I have? _____

2. Education and training

What education and training are needed? _____

_____

What education and training will I have when I complete high school? _____

_____

What education and training will I be able to obtain after high school? _____

_____

3. Work Setting

What is the work setting like? _____

What type of work setting do I prefer? _____

4. Hours

What hours are required? _____

What hours do I prefer? _____

5. Duties and Responsibilities

What are the responsibilities? _____

_____

What responsibilities do I prefer? _____

_____

6. Personality characteristics

What type of personality would be successful? _____

What type of personality do I have? _____

7. Location

Where is the work located? _____

What location do I prefer? _____

8. Advancement

What are the advancement opportunities? _____

What advancement do I look forward to? _____

Continued on next page

9. Job outlook

What is the job outlook? _____

Will there be jobs available for me? _____

10. What is the expected pay in this career? _____

Will this pay match what I would like to receive? _____

Critical Thinking

1. Did the 10 descriptions of the job frequently match your preferences?
For example, is the location where you prefer? Is the pay what you want?
List all the matches.

The things about Career #1 that match my needs: _____

_____

The things about Career #2 that match my needs: _____

_____

2. List the differences.

The things about Career #1 that do not match my needs: _____

_____

The things about Career #2 that do not match my needs: _____

_____

3. Are there more matches or more differences? _____

Explain what you have learned about how you and these careers match: _____

_____

_____

_____

_____

_____

_____

_____

_____

CHAPTER 4 Making Career Decisions

ACTIVITY 1 *Decision-Making Practice*

for use with Lesson 4.1

Your Goal: Practice the seven steps in good decision making.

What to Do: Read the following case study about Patricia's decision. Then analyze Patricia's decision-making skills.

Patricia's Decision

Patricia needed to make some money while she was still in school. She and her parents decided Patricia should earn her spending money. She also wanted to save money for her college expenses. She wanted to eventually work in some area of health care.

Patricia was talking to her friend Juan one day. She told him she was looking for a job after school and on Saturdays. Juan told her that he had heard there were a lot of part-time jobs around town. He knew that Speedy Burger was looking for people.

Patricia went to Speedy Burger and got a job cleaning tables. It wasn't her first choice for a job, but she figured any job would do.

After working at Speedy Burger a few months, Patricia wasn't happy. She didn't like the job she was assigned. She didn't think the employer would let her change to any other job at Speedy Burger, and her present job was not helping her learn about health care. "Oh well," Patricia thought, "There's nothing I can do now."

Analyze Patricia's Decision

Patricia made a decision about taking a part-time job. However, the decision did not turn out well. How could Patricia have improved the decision-making process?

The seven steps in the decision-making process are listed on the next page. For each step, write a minimum of one suggestion that would have helped Patricia make a better decision. Refer to your textbook for an explanation of each step in decision making.

Continued on next page

Chapter 4 • Exploring Careers

Steps in Decision Making	Suggestions for Patricia
1. Define your needs or wants.	
2. Analyze your resources.	
3. Identify your options.	
4. Gather information.	
5. Evaluate your options.	
6. Make a decision.	
7. Plan how to reach your goal.	

CHAPTER 4   Making Career Decisions

ACTIVITY 2   *Your Decision-Making Ability*

for use with Lesson 4.1

Your Goal: Analyze your own decision-making ability.

What to Do: First make a list of some of the decisions you have
made this week, this month, and this year. You don't have to list all of the
decisions. Just write the first ones that come to mind. Then rate yourself
as a decision maker.

My Decisions

Decisions I have made this week:
(For example, visiting a friend instead of going to a movie.)

_____

_____

_____

_____

Decisions I have made this month:
(For example, I decided to volunteer one afternoon a month at the local hospital.)

_____

_____

_____

_____

Decisions I have made this year:
(For example, I decided to take geometry next year instead of basic math.)

_____

_____

_____

_____

Continued on next page

How I Rate as a Decision Maker

Evaluate yourself. Rate yourself as a decision maker. Answer the following questions by putting a check next to *usually, sometimes,* or *rarely*. Then answer the Critical Thinking questions.

1. Do you define what your needs and wants are before you make a decision?

☐ Usually   ☐ Sometimes   ☐ Rarely

Explain:

_____

_____

_____

2. Do you analyze the resources you have available to help you make a decision?

☐ Usually   ☐ Sometimes   ☐ Rarely

Explain:

_____

_____

_____

_____

3. Do you look at all possible options or choices before you make a decision?

☐ Usually   ☐ Sometimes   ☐ Rarely

Explain:

_____

_____

_____

_____

4. Do you gather information about all of the different options before you make a decision?

☐ Usually   ☐ Sometimes   ☐ Rarely

Explain:

_____

_____

_____

_____

5. Do you evaluate all of those options before making a decision?

☐ Usually ☐ Sometimes ☐ Rarely

Explain:

_____

_____

_____

_____

6. Are you able to make a decision with confidence?

☐ Usually ☐ Sometimes ☐ Rarely

Explain:

_____

_____

_____

_____

7. After you make a decision, do you make a plan of action to reach your goal?

☐ Usually ☐ Sometimes ☐ Rarely

Explain:

_____

_____

_____

_____

8. Do you find it easy to make a decision?

☐ Usually ☐ Sometimes ☐ Rarely

Explain:

_____

_____

_____

_____

Continued on next page

9. Are you satisfied with the decisions you make?

☐ Usually ☐ Sometimes ☐ Rarely

Explain:

_____

_____

_____

_____

10. Do you like making decisions?

☐ Usually ☐ Sometimes ☐ Rarely

Explain:

_____

_____

_____

_____

Critical Thinking

1. Using your answers to the questions on decision making, analyze your decision-making ability. Write one or two sentences describing yourself as a decision maker.

_____

_____

_____

_____

_____

2. How can you improve your decision-making ability?

_____

_____

_____

_____

_____

_____

CHAPTER 4 Making Career Decisions

File in your Career Resource File.

ACTIVITY 3 *Deciding on Your Career Path*

for use with Lesson 4.2

Your Goal: Make a tentative choice of a career path to follow.

What to Do: Use the seven decision-making steps listed below. These are the same steps you used to evaluate Patricia's decision in Activity 1. Using this process will help you decide which career path to follow.

Steps in the Decision-Making Process

Step 1: What do I need or want?
What general career cluster do you want to pursue? Career clusters are listed in Activity 1 in Chapter 3.

_____

_____

Step 2: What resources will help me decide?
Do you have resources that will help you meet your needs? You have identified resources such as your skills and aptitudes, interests, values, and personality characteristics. List those below. Also, what other resources do you have to help you on your career path?

_____

_____

_____

_____

Step 3: What occupations in my career cluster seem interesting?

_____

_____

_____

_____

_____

Continued on next page

Chapter 4 • Exploring Careers 47

Step 4: What can I find out about them?

List the advantages and disadvantages of each occupation in your career cluster.

_____

_____

_____

_____

Step 5: Which occupation seems best for me?

Rank or prioritize your choices as first, second, third, etc.

_____

_____

_____

_____

Step 6: What's my decision?

_____

_____

_____

_____

Step 7: How can I reach my career goal?

What can you do, starting today, to achieve your career goal? Write down everything that comes to mind.

_____

_____

_____

_____

_____

_____

_____

CHAPTER 4 Making Career Decisions

ACTIVITY 4 *Looking at Goal Setting*
for use with Lesson 4.2

Your Goal: Analyze someone else's ability to set goals.

What to Do: Read the following story about Ray. How good was Ray at setting and meeting his career goals? Rate Ray's plan of action.

Ray's Story

   Ray wanted to manage a recreation center some day. He knew this wouldn't happen right away. He figured if he worked hard enough, his dream would come true.

   Ray had always been good in almost all sports. He worked out several times a week and stayed in good condition. Ray spent his spare time in the school gym. So did most of his friends.

   Ray read the sports pages and sports magazines and watched sports on TV. Sports occupied most of Ray's life.

   He was an average student and usually tried his best. Teachers could rely on Ray to do what he promised.

   Ray had a summer job on a landscaping crew. He made pretty good money. He knew his parents couldn't pay for his college education, so he hoped to save money for his education. He was also wondering whether he could get a scholarship. Ray didn't know what he would have to do to work in sports recreation. He figured he would find out more when he got to college.

Ray's Plan

Analyze Ray's goal-setting ability:

1. In which career cluster is Ray's career path? What is his specific goal?

_____

_____

_____

_____

Continued on next page

2. What is his plan of action?

_____

_____

_____

3. What obstacles might Ray have to overcome?

_____

_____

_____

Critical Thinking

1. Does Ray have well-defined goals?

☐ Yes   ☐ No

Explain: _____

_____

2. Does Ray have the qualifications to meet his goals?

☐ Yes   ☐ No

Explain: _____

_____

3. Does Ray have a well-developed plan for reaching his career goals?

☐ Yes   ☐ No

Explain: _____

_____

4. Is Ray doing everything he can to meet his goals?

☐ Yes   ☐ No

Explain: _____

_____

5. Should Ray be re-evaluating his plan of action for his future?

☐ Yes   ☐ No

Explain: _____

_____

CHAPTER 4 Making Career Decisions

ACTIVITY 5   *Making Your Predictions*

for use with Lesson 4.2

Your Goal: Match people with possible career choices.

What to Do: Try your hand at matching people with careers they might be suited for. Read each of the descriptions in this activity. Then suggest one or more careers each person would probably like. Give reasons for your answer.

What Should Sam Do?

Sam is a person who always takes care of every detail. He is good in math and usually helps his friends with their math problems. There doesn't seem to be a math problem too hard for Sam to tackle.

Sam doesn't mind being alone. He can spend hours working on his brother's bicycle. Sometimes his friends come over to play basketball. Sam is well-liked and easy to get along with.

On Saturdays and after school, Sam works in a local supermarket. He stocks shelves and helps the assistant store manager with inventory reports. When Sam does the inventory reports, he is careful with the details. He knows how important it is to be accurate.

Sam has considered three careers: becoming a business owner, an accountant, or a math teacher.

What careers would you choose for Sam?   Give reasons for these choices.

First choice _____   _____

Second choice _____   _____

Continued on next page

Chapter 4 • Exploring Careers   51

What Should Maria Do?

Everyone says Maria is a natural athlete. She's the star forward on the basketball team, and in outdoor track, she runs the 200 meter in 26 seconds and the 400 meter in 60 seconds. When school is closed, Maria jogs with her friends several days a week.

Maria is careful about what she eats. She has read that eating the right foods is as important for an athlete as having ability.

Lately Maria has become interested in computers. She's taking a computer course and is doing very well. She has been talking to her teacher about all of the possible uses of computers. She has been wondering how computers and sports can work together.

Maria has been thinking about three careers: Physical Education teacher, dietitian, and Webmaster for an athletic team's Web site.

What careers would you choose for Maria? Give reasons for these choices.

First choice _____

Second choice _____

What Should Evelyn Do?

Evelyn is an average student. She gets Bs and Cs in her classes at school. Evelyn has always been able to see the way things fit together. When she was a small child, she could put puzzle pieces together quickly. At home she is always curious about how everything works. Lately she has spent a lot of time with her father and older brother working on the family car. She enjoys doing this and has learned a lot.

Evelyn spends a lot of time reading. Now she is reading science fiction and has become interested in space travel. Evelyn spends a lot of time thinking about what is in space.

Evelyn has been thinking about three careers: an auto-emissions specialist, an astronomer, or an astronaut.

What careers would you choose for Evelyn? Give reasons for these choices.

First choice _____

Second choice _____

File in
your Career
Resource File.

CHAPTER 5 Planning Your Career

Your Goal: Find out about the types of training and education you might need to meet your career goal.

What to Do: Listed below are education and training choices you may have after you graduate from high school. Decide which of these will help you meet your career goal.

My career goal is _____

1. Put a check next to each type of education and training that would be helpful to you. Write N/A (not applicable) next to those that would not be helpful to you.

_____ On-the-Job Training (training in a particular job right on the job)

_____ Apprenticeship (hands-on experience in a job under the guidance of a skilled worker)

_____ Vocational-Technical Centers (skills-training programs in areas such as automotive or computer technology)

_____ Trade Schools (training for particular professions, such as hair styling, truck driving, or cooking)

_____ Community and Technical Colleges (Associate degree for two-year program in areas such as accounting or certificate in areas such as court reporting)

_____ Four-Year Colleges and Universities (Bachelor's degree for four years of study and advanced degrees beyond four years)

_____ Military Service (training in more than 200 jobs, including health technician and air-traffic controller)

_____ Continuing Education (courses and programs that help adults complete education, brush up old skills, pursue new interests)

_____ Distance Education (online classes for specific training or for credit towards a degree)

Continued on next page

2. Select one of the schools or training centers from the list above. Locate three schools of that type that you might be able to attend. For each school, list as much of the following information as possible.

Name of school #1: _____

Special entrance requirements: _____

I plan to study: _____

Type of training needed: _____

Length of time needed to finish training: _____

Approximate cost per year (or session): _____

Approximate cost of special equipment needed: _____

Name of school #2: _____

Special entrance requirements: _____

I plan to study: _____

Type of training needed: _____

Length of time needed to finish training: _____

Approximate cost per year (or session): _____

Approximate cost of special equipment needed: _____

Name of school #3: _____

Special entrance requirements: _____

I plan to study: _____

Type of training needed: _____

Length of time needed to finish training: _____

Approximate cost per year (or session): _____

Approximate cost of special equipment needed: _____

Critical Thinking

Compare the information you have gathered on the schools.

1. Which school would you choose? Why? _____

_____

2. How would you pay for the training? _____

_____

3. What age would you be when you finished your training? _____

CHAPTER 5 Planning Your Career

File in your Career Resource File.

ACTIVITY 2   *Developing a Planning Sheet*

for use with Lesson 5.2

Your Goal: Develop a planning sheet to give you direction on your career path.

What to Do: Fill in the information below about your plans for high school and for post-high school education and training. "Post-high school" means what you will do after you graduate from high school.

My career choice is _____

High School

List the courses you will need to take in high school for admission to post-high school education and training. Refer to the previous exercise in which you listed "special entrance requirements" for three schools.

_____

_____

Post-High School Education and Training

List the type of post-high school education or training you will need for your career choice. Again, refer to the previous exercise in which you listed the training needed for your career choice.

Type of education or training needed: _____

_____

Approximate length of time to complete course of study: _____

_____

Jobs Leading Toward Career Goals

List any jobs that can help you to reach your career goals. These may include part-time jobs, full-time jobs, temporary jobs, and volunteer experiences.

Part-time jobs: _____

_____

Continued on next page

Full-time jobs: _____

_____

Temporary jobs: _____

_____

Volunteer experiences, including job shadowing and internships: _____

_____

Personal Obligations/Duties

List any obligations or duties that could cause you to alter or change your plans. For example, you may need to care for your younger brother after school. If you can't think of any obligation or duty, write "none."

_____

_____

_____

_____

Dates

Read back over the information you have just completed in this exercise. Write the dates when you plan to begin and complete each one. (Some dates may overlap, such as part-time jobs and schooling.) Be realistic about what you hope to accomplish. Take into consideration any personal obligations and duties noted above.

Experience	Start Date	Finish Date
High School		
Post-High School Education and Training		
Part-time Job Leading to Career Goals		
Full-time Job Leading to Career Goals		
Temporary Job Leading to Career Goals		
Volunteer Job Leading to Career Goals		

CHAPTER 5 Planning Your Career

File in your Career Resource File.

ACTIVITY 3   *Your Career Plan*

for use with Lesson 5.2

Your Goal: Organize your short-, medium-, and long-term goals.

What to Do: You will be setting three long-term goals, with short- and medium-term goals before them. On the lines below, first write your long-term goal. Then decide what medium- and short-term goals you need to accomplish before you can get to your long-term goal.

Then fill in the Chart of Career Goals to indicate the dates when you will begin and complete your goals.

Example:

Long-term goal: go to a university

Medium-term goal: get money to go to university

Short-term goal: finish high school with good grades

Long-term goal #1: _____

Medium-term goal: _____

Short-term goal: _____

Long-term goal #2: _____

Medium-term goal: _____

Short-term goal: _____

Long-term goal #3: _____

Medium-term goal: _____

Short-term goal: _____

Continued on next page

Chart of Career Goals

Career Goal/Notes	Goal: Short-, Medium-, or Long-term	Dates	
		Begin	Complete
1.			
2.			
3.			
4.			
5.			
6.			
7.			
8.			
9.			
10.			

CHAPTER **5** Planning Your Career

ACTIVITY 4	*Key Terms in Planning*

for use with Lesson 5.2

Your Goal: Learn the key terms you need for making your career plan.

What to Do: Unscramble the words that match the definitions in the second column.

Key Words Scramble

Key Word	Definition
T R O C P R A S N I T E A	to put off deciding or doing something
R O I I P R I Z E T	to put tasks in order of importance
T A R P M I T E B O J	work up to 30 hours a week
M E T P O R A R Y O B J	work for a short time
L U F L M I T E B O J	work 40 hours a week
T H O R S M E R T L O A G	something you might start right away to help toward your long-term goal
D E M I U M T R M E A G O L	a goal in between your short-term goal and your long-term goal
N O L G M E R T L O G A	your ultimate or final goal
L O G I C A L R C H O N O D O R E R	the order in which things happen

Continued on next page

Critical Thinking

1. Pretend that you are planning a party. Describe your preparations for the party using at least five of the key terms listed on the previous page.

_____

_____

_____

_____

_____

_____

_____

_____

2. Describe how internships, part-time jobs, temporary jobs, and full-time jobs can help you in achieving your own long-term career goals.

_____

_____

_____

_____

_____

_____

_____

_____

CHAPTER 6 Finding a Job

File in your Career Resource File.

ACTIVITY 1 *Job Leads*
for use with Lesson 6.1

Your Goal: Discover how to find part-time, temporary, or volunteer jobs by using job leads.

What to Do: Complete the information for each of the items below.

1. Sources for job leads are listed below. Put a check next to the sources you plan to investigate.

   _____ Cooperative program at school

   _____ Service learning program in the community

   _____ Job/Volunteer listings at school

   _____ Job/Volunteer leads in the newspaper

   _____ Job/Volunteer leads on radio or TV

   _____ Job leads from calling businesses listed in the *Yellow Pages*

   _____ Job leads found out by talking to people such as counselors at school or people in the work world. This is called networking.

   Other: _____

2. What part-time or volunteer jobs are available? How did you find out about these jobs? Do you qualify for them? Use the following chart to answer these questions.

Job	Source of Lead	Am I Qualified?
1.		
2.		
3.		
4.		
5.		

Continued on next page

Critical Thinking

What could you learn from getting a part-time or volunteer job? Take two of the possible jobs from the list on the previous page and describe how you would benefit from having those jobs.

Job title #1: _____

_____

How I would benefit/what I would learn: _____

_____

_____

_____

_____

_____

_____

_____

Job title #2: _____

_____

How I would benefit/what I would learn: _____

_____

_____

CHAPTER **6** Finding a Job

ACTIVITY 2   *Reading the Classified Ads*

for use with Lesson 6.1

Your Goal: Learn how to read classified advertisements for job openings.

What to Do: Following are some classified ads that appeared in a newspaper. Read each ad. Then answer the questions for each one.

EXEC. SECY
Local Corp. Headquarters seeks Exec. Secy to work for VP of Sales. Indiv should have exec skills and be able to work independ. Excel starting salary and oppty for growth. For appt. call:
SMITH RESOURCES INC.
555-0130
Personnel Consultants   Fee $5

1. What is the title of the position? _____

2. What are the qualifications for the job? _____

_____

3. Who is the employer? _____

FITNESS INSTRUCTOR
Approx. 14-16 hours per week. Aerobics teaching experience required. Must be outgoing and enjoy helping people. Nautilus & free weight experience desirable. Work schedule requires flexibility for weekends. Apply in person to Don Autzen at The Metro Club, 555-0111.

1. What is the work schedule? _____

2. What experience is needed? _____

3. How do you apply? _____

NURSES AIDES, HOME HEALTH AIDES
—Part-time positions available, 8 to 12 noon and 9 AM to 1 PM and 10 AM to 2 PM, weekdays and/or weekends in a growing home health agency. Will train those sincerely interested & dedicated. Help make a difference in someone's life & yet still have that precious time to devote to your own. To become a valued member of our respected health care team call 888-0909, 9 to 4:30 M-F for an appt. 555-0189.

1. What is the work schedule? _____

_____

2. What training do you need? _____

3. What are the benefits of the job? _____

_____

4. How do you apply? _____

PART TIME $7–$8/HOUR
Plus commission. Telephone sales. Expr pref'd. Will train. Mon-Fri 5 PM-8 PM. Call Marilyn 555-0172 10 AM-6 PM.

1. What is the salary? _____

2. What is the type of work? _____

3. How do you apply? _____

Continued on next page

PICTURE FRAMING
Growing company looking for people to work in custom picture frame shop. Must be detail oriented, dependable and have good math skills. Training available. Good benefit package. Full-time, Mon. through Fri.
Apply in person:
STOTT'S ARTIST SUPPLIES
5515 Holly View
Cincinnati, OH 45454

1. What are the qualifications for the job? _____
_____

2. What does "training available" mean? _____
_____

3. How do you apply? _____

WORD PROCESSOR — Part-time/permanent position. Great opportunity to work in Dickerson Marketing Co. in the evening. 4 PM to 9 PM or 5 PM to 10 PM (hours are somewhat flexible). Exp. on any word processor will qualify you for this job. Must be able to type 60 wpm. $9.00/Hr. Call Designaide 555-0167. (Fee Paid by Client Company).

1. What is the type of position? _____

2. What are the hours? _____

3. What experience do you need? _____
_____

4. Who pays the fee for finding the job? _____
_____

FULL- & PART-TIME
Luigi's Pizza is looking for mature responsible people who would like to be part of a winning team. $7 per hr guaranteed for the 1st 2 wks—potential to earn as high as $10–$12 per hr. Apply at any Luigi's Pizza loc. for personal or confidential interview call 555-0199. Min. age 18 w/own transportation. Luigi's Pizza is an equal oppty employer.

1. What is the salary? _____

2. Where do you apply? _____

3. What are the qualifications for the job? _____
_____

CHAPTER **6** Finding a Job

File in your Career Resource File.

ACTIVITY 3   *A Job That Might Interest You*

for use with Lesson 6.1

Your Goal: Evaluate a job in a classified ad.

What to Do: Look through the classified ads in your newspaper. Locate one ad for a job that you think you are qualified for. Clip the ad and attach it in the space provided below. Answer the questions that follow about the ad and how you would follow it up.

The Classified Ad I Found:

1. What does the ad say about the job? Answer as many of the following questions as possible. If the information is not in the ad, write N/A (not applicable).

    What is the title of the position? _____

    _____

    What are the duties? _____

    _____

    What are the qualifications for the job? _____

    _____

    What is the wage or salary? _____

    _____

    How do you apply for the job? _____

    _____

Continued on next page

2. Is there anything else you want to know about the job? Write down your questions.

_____

_____

_____

3. What information would you want to know about the employer?

_____

_____

_____

4. How would you find information about the employer?

_____

_____

_____

Critical Thinking

1. Why do you think you are qualified for the job? Refer to the information you have already organized about your skills, aptitudes, and experience.

_____

_____

_____

2. Are there any qualifications you do not have? If you answer yes, list them.

_____

_____

_____

_____

3. How could you compensate (make up) for the qualifications that you don't have?

_____

_____

_____

_____

CHAPTER **6** Finding a Job

ACTIVITY 4   *Telephone Contacts*

for use with Lesson 6.1

Your Goal: Identify the strong points in a telephone conversation by a job-seeker.

What to Do: Read the telephone contact Brian had with Mr. LaRusso asking about a job opening. Then fill in the information in the spaces provided.

Brian's Conversation

"Hello, my name is Brian Edwards. I would like to speak to the manager. I think his name is Mr. LaRusso. Is that right? Thank you."

"Mr. LaRusso, I'm Brian Edwards. A friend of mine, Mike Provost, told me you are hiring people to work after school and on weekends as checkers and shelf stockers in the store. I am looking for a part-time job now, and I could work those times."

"Yes, I have some work experience. For the past two summers, I did landscaping work for the Lawn Ranger Landscaping Company. Mr. Lopez was my boss. If you would like to call him, I can give you his telephone number."

"Even though I haven't worked in a store before, I know I would learn fast. I learned a lot when I worked with the landscaping company. Mr. Lopez gave me two raises while I worked there. I know he liked the job I did. I asked him about work now, but he's only hiring full-time people."

"Yes, I can come in to talk with you. Monday at four would be fine. Thank you for talking to me. I'm looking forward to meeting you."

Your Feedback to Brian

Identify at least six strong points of Brian's conversation with Mr. LaRusso.

1. _____

_____

_____

_____

_____

_____

Continued on next page

2.

3.

4.

5.

6.

CHAPTER **6** Finding a Job

ACTIVITY 5   *How to Look for a Job*

for use with Lesson 6.2

Your Goal: Evaluate Frank's job-search methods and suggest ways he could organize his search.

What to Do: Read the following conversation between Frank and Bill. After reading the conversation, suggest how Frank could organize his search for a job.

Frank and Bill's Conversation

Frank: Looking around for a job is really getting me down. How come other people find jobs and I can't?

Bill: I don't know, Frank. I don't see what's the matter with you. Where have you looked?

Frank: Well, I read the classified ads. They had some part-time jobs, but I'm not sure I'm qualified for them. I think they're looking for someone with more experience.

Bill: That's too bad. I think anyone would be lucky to have you work for their business. You've had some part-time jobs before. Wouldn't any of those experiences help you now?

Frank: No, I don't know if they would help. Well, maybe if I hang in there, something will turn up. How did you find your job?

Bill: My brother heard about it and thought I ought to apply. For me, getting a lead about a job wasn't as hard as filling out the job application. It took me forever to find the information they wanted—schools I went to, other jobs, references.

Frank: I don't have that information either. Well, I don't need it anyway since I don't have any job leads.

Continued on next page

Your Suggestions to Frank for Organizing His Job Search

Write six suggestions you would make to Frank to organize his job search.
For each suggestion, write two or three sentences explaining what Frank might
do to make that suggestion pay off. Refer to your textbook for suggestions.

1. _____

   _____

   _____

2. _____

   _____

   _____

3. _____

   _____

   _____

4. _____

   _____

   _____

5. _____

   _____

   _____

6. _____

   _____

   _____

CHAPTER 7 Applying for a Job

ACTIVITY 1 *Looking at Résumés*

for use with Lesson 7.1

Your Goal: Learn to identify weaknesses in a résumé.

What to Do: Read the following résumé. Then make suggestions for improving Kiki's résumé.

"Kiki" Johnson
171 Edge Place
Fairfield, CT 06430

Employment Goal: Ten years from now I want to be a buyer for a large department store.

Experience: Working at Hemlock
Department Store
Like stock car racing
I also like to fish

Education: Go to Ward High School

References: Loretta Johnson
(my mother)

Continued on next page

Your Suggestions for Kiki

In the spaces provided below, list six ways Kiki's résumé can be improved.

1. _____
   _____
   _____
   _____

2. _____
   _____
   _____

3. _____
   _____
   _____
   _____

4. _____
   _____
   _____

5. _____
   _____
   _____

6. _____
   _____
   _____
   _____

CHAPTER 7 Applying for a Job

File in your Career Resource File.

Your Goal: Gather the information to write two kinds of résumés for your job search: a chronological and a skills résumé.

What to Do: You are going to gather together the information to write your own résumés. You may want to use your lists of interests, hobbies, skills and aptitudes that you made in previous activities in this workbook.

Both résumés will start with your name, address, and phone number, followed by the job objective (the job applied for). After that information, follow the headings below.

Then decide which résumé would make you look the best to an employer and what you could do to improve your own résumé.

Skills Résumé

The skills résumé puts the main emphasis on your skills and abilities rather than on your work experience.

Fill in the following to help you to write a skills résumé:

Name: _____

Address: _____

Phone Number: _____

Job Objective: _____

Skills and Abilities: _____

_____

_____

Education: _____

Honors and Activities: _____

_____

_____

References: _____

_____

Continued on next page

Chronological Résumé

A chronological résumé puts the emphasis on your work experience. List all work experience, including volunteering, in reverse order. Start with the most recent experience.

Name: _____

Address: _____

Phone Number: _____

Job Objective: _____

Work Experience: _____

_____

Education: _____

Honors and Activities: _____

_____

_____

Special Skills and Abilities: _____

_____

_____

References: _____

_____

_____

Critical Thinking

1. Which type of résumé would you use to make you look the best to an employer—a chronological or skills résumé?

_____

_____

2. Give three reasons why you would choose that type of résumé format.

_____

_____

3. What could you do to add more to your résumé? List five things you could start today to improve the information on your résumé. For example, "I could take a computer or a typing class."

_____

_____

CHAPTER 7 Applying for a Job

Writing Letters About Jobs

for use with Lesson 7.1

Your Goal: Analyze a letter to an employer about job openings.

What to Do: Read the following letter written by Cynthia. Then sharpen your letter-writing skills by pointing out where she could improve.

Cynthia's Letter

Mrs. Garza,
Specialty Company
171 North Main
Little Rock, AK

Dear Mrs. Garza,

I heard you will have some part-time jobs.
I hope you will keep an opening for me.

I am going to Thornton High school. I will
graduate next year. This year I am looking
for a part-time job. I can work after school
and on the weekends. I have not worked
before. I think my teachers like my work.

I would be able to come to speak to you
any day after school.

Love,

Cynthia Wall
Cynthia Wall

Continued on next page

Chapter 7 • Exploring Careers 75

Your Suggestions to Cynthia

Identify at least five ways Cynthia can improve the letter she wrote to
Mrs. Garza.

1. _____

_____

_____

_____

2. _____

_____

_____

_____

3. _____

_____

_____

_____

4. _____

_____

_____

_____

5. _____

_____

_____

_____

CHAPTER 7 Applying for a Job

File in your Career Resource File.

ACTIVITY 4   *Writing a Cover Letter*

for use with Lesson 7.1

Your Goal: Learn to write an effective cover letter to match your résumé.

What to Do: Look at the sample cover letter below. Then create your own letter to go with the résumé that you wrote in Activity 2.

Sample Cover Letter

> 48 South Elgin Street
> Merryville, ME 96780
>
>
> May 4, 20––
>
> Mr. Frederick Rasat
> Director
> Mercy Hospital
> 4832 Grand Avenue
> Merryville, ME 96780
>
> Dear Mr. Rasat:
>
> I am a 10th grade student at Rosemont High School and would like to volunteer in a hospital during my summer break. My counselor suggested that I apply to Mercy Hospital because of the good volunteer training that you offer.
>
> My reason for wanting to volunteer in a hospital is that I am planning to train as a Registered Nurse after I graduate from high school. I want to learn all I can before I start my training. As I said in my résumé, I have worked on the local Blood Drive and belong to Future Nurses of America. I also have experience caring for my neighbor's three children.
>
> I am hoping you will schedule me for an interview at your convenience. My phone number is 444-555-0165. Thank you for your consideration. I look forward to meeting you.
>
> Sincerely,
>
> *Maria Tosar*
> Maria Tosar

Continued on next page

Your Own Cover Letter

Now is the time to write your own cover letter. Your letter should have three parts:

- **Opening:** Introduce yourself. State the job you are applying for and how you found out about it.
- **Body:** Sell yourself. Describe your skills and experience that fit the job. Mention that you are sending a résumé.
- **Closing:** Ask for an interview. Include your phone number and thank the person you are writing to for his or her time and interest.

Now, write your letter in the space provided below:

_____

_____

_____

_____

_____

_____

_____

_____

_____

_____

_____

_____

_____

_____

_____

Critical Thinking

Pretend that you are an employer. Evaluate your own letter. Would you hire the person writing this letter? Why or why not?

_____

_____

_____

_____

CHAPTER **7** Applying for a Job

File in your Career Resource File.

ACTIVITY 5 *Completing Application Forms*

for use with Lesson 7.1

Your Goal: Practice completing application forms as neatly and accurately as possible.

What to Do: Take the time to practice "the art" of completing application forms. Use pencil before you complete the application in ink or use a rough copy.

Always write N/A in any blank for which an answer is not required. N/A means "Not Applicable" and tells the employer that you saw the question, but it does not apply to you.

Fill in the two sample applications. Then answer the Critical Thinking questions that follow.

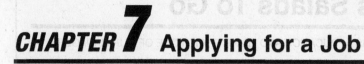

Continued on next page

Sam's Salads To Go

COMPLETE THIS APPLICATION AND LEAVE IT WITH ONE OF OUR MANAGERS

NAME _____ SOCIAL SECURITY # _____

ADDRESS _____ CITY _____ STATE _____

TEL. # _____ PREVIOUS EXPERIENCE WITH SAM'S SALADS _____

HOW FAR FROM THIS STORE DO YOU LIVE? _____ HOW WOULD YOU GET HERE? _____

HOW MANY HOURS A WEEK WOULD YOU LIKE TO WORK? _____ COULD YOU WORK DURING SCHOOL HRS.? _____

COULD YOU WORK AFTER 10:00 P.M.? _____

PLEASE FILL IN THE HOURS YOU ARE AVAILABLE

	SATURDAY	SUNDAY	MONDAY	TUESDAY	WEDNESDAY	THURSDAY	FRIDAY
FROM							
UNTIL							

LAST SCHOOL ATTENDED _____ UNTIL _____ YEAR GRADUATED _____

SPORTS OR ACTIVITIES _____

MOST RECENT EMPLOYER

    NAME _____ DATES OF EMPLOYMENT FROM _____

    ADDRESS _____ UNTIL _____

    _____

    TEL. # _____

    NAME OF MANAGER _____

APPLICATION FOR EMPLOYMENT

SUPERIOR MARKETS

DIRECTIONS: Please use a pen and print.
Answer all sections completely and accurately.

NAME			SOCIAL SECURITY NUMBER
LAST	FIRST	MIDDLE	___ ___ ___ – ___ ___ – ___ ___ ___ ___

HOME ADDRESS				
NUMBER STREET		CITY	STATE	ZIP

HOME TELEPHONE #	ALTERNATE TELEPHONE#

POSITION APPLIED FOR	SPECIFY DAYS AND HOURS AVAILABLE	PAY DESIRED

EDUCATION

	NAME AND ADDRESS OF SCHOOL	COURSE	DATE LEFT
ELEMENTARY			
MIDDLE SCHOOL			
HIGH SCHOOL			
VOCATIONAL SCHOOL			
COLLEGE OR UNIVERSITY			
OTHER			

LAST EMPLOYMENT

NAME OF COMPANY	ADDRESS	SUPERVISOR	JOB	PAY

DATE BEGAN	DATE LEFT	REASON FOR LEAVING

Additional qualifications applicant has to offer for consideration. These may include job-related interests, experiences, or volunteer activities.

_____

_____

_____

_____

The facts set forth on my application are true and complete.

DATE _____ SIGNATURE _____

Continued on next page

Critical Thinking

1. Were there any questions that you could not answer? If so, list the questions below.

_____

_____

_____

_____

_____

2. Where would you go to get the answers to those questions? Explain how you would find the answers to those questions.

_____

_____

_____

_____

_____

3. Pretend that you own Sam's Salads or are the manager of Superior Markets. Look over your two applications. How do they look? Would you hire you? Why or why not?

_____

_____

_____

_____

_____

_____

CHAPTER 7 Applying For a Job

Improving Interview Skills

for use with Lesson 7.2

Your Goal: Learn to analyze strengths and weaknesses in a person's interviewing style.

What to Do: Read the descriptions that follow and analyze Lee's approach to interviewing.

Lee Prepares for the Interview

Lee really wants a job at Hardy's Hardware. After he graduates from high school, he wants to work in the construction industry. His dream is to have his own business as a building contractor. He knows he will have to start as a carpenter's apprentice and learn all that he can.

Lee thinks it will be good experience to work in a hardware store while he is in school. He called the manager of Hardy's and made an appointment for an interview. A friend of his had been on a job interview, so Lee talked to him about his interview. This helped Lee know what to expect on the interview.

Lee's interview was after school at four o'clock. He tried to be careful about the way he dressed. He knew that the sales people in the hardware stores usually dressed casually. After Lee took a shower, he put on his best slacks and sport shirt.

Lee had to speak to a friend after school, and it made him five minutes late for the interview. He didn't think that five minutes would make that much difference. When he got to the store, he asked for Mr. Gomez, the manager.

The Interview

Mr. Gomez came out of the stockroom and invited Lee to sit down so they could talk.

Mr. Gomez: "Well, Lee, why are you so interested in working in the hardware business?"

Lee: "Mr. Gomez, I want to learn as much as I can about the building business. I want to train to become a carpenter and own my own building business some day. I thought that the more I found out about building and home repair, the more certain I could be about what I wanted to do. My mom and dad both work on repairing our house, and I learn from them when they're working. I really like carpentry work so far."

Mr. Gomez: "That sounds good to me. How do you do at school? What kind of grades do you make and what are your other interests?"

Lee: "I'm a pretty good student. I usually get mostly Bs and a few Cs. I like school. I have a lot of friends there."

Mr. Gomez: "What do you know about the hardware business?"

Continued on next page

Lee: "Well, I go to the hardware store with my parents when they shop for supplies. I look around the store, so I know about a lot of the supplies. I'd really like a part-time job, and I know I'll catch on fast. I can work after school and on weekends. My parents think my getting a job is a good idea."

Mr. Gomez: "Who could I call as a reference to find out more about you?"

Lee: "I'm not sure. I guess you could talk to my mom and dad."

Mr. Gomez: "Is there anyone else I could talk to who knows how you might work out here?"

Lee: "Not that I can think of now."

Mr. Gomez: "OK, Lee. Thanks for coming to talk with me. We'll see what we can do."

Lee: "It's been nice talking to you, Mr. Gomez."

Your Suggestions to Lee

Analyze Lee's interview and the way he prepared for it. In the spaces provided, list at least three of Lee's strengths and three of his weaknesses.

Lee's Strengths

_____

_____

_____

Lee's Weaknesses

_____

_____

_____

In the spaces provided below, list at least three ways that Lee can improve his interviewing skills.

_____

_____

_____

Critical Thinking

Do you think Lee got the job at Hardy's Hardware? Explain below why you think he did or did not get the job.

_____

_____

_____

_____

CHAPTER 7 Applying For a Job

ACTIVITY 7 *How Do They Rate?*

for use with Lesson 7.2

Your Goal: Learn to recognize and evaluate nonverbal behavior.

What to Do: Following are illustrations of nonverbal behaviors. Pretend you are the employer interviewing these people. What do you think these behaviors are saying?

Next to each number, check whether the behavior seems to be positive (☺) or negative (☹) and write your comments about what the behavior says to you. Then check whether each person prepared well or could have prepared better. Suggest ways each poorly prepared person could have prepared better in order to avoid the negative behavior.

1. ☺ _____ or ☹ _____

☐ This person prepared well.

☐ This person could have prepared better by:

_____

_____

What the person's behavior seems to be saying:

_____

_____

_____

_____

_____

_____

Continued on next page

2. ☺ _____ or ☹ _____

What the person's behavior seems to be saying:

_____

_____

_____

_____

_____

_____

_____

☐ This person prepared well.

☐ This person could have prepared better by:

_____

_____

3. ☺ _____ or ☹ _____

What the person's behavior seems to be saying:

_____

_____

_____

_____

_____

_____

_____

_____

_____

☐ This person prepared well.

☐ This person could have prepared better by:

_____

_____

(Continued on next page)

4. ☺ _____ or ☹ _____

What the person's behavior seems to be saying:

_____
_____
_____
_____
_____
_____
_____

☐ This person prepared well.

☐ This person could have prepared better by:

_____
_____

5. ☺ _____ or ☹ _____

What the person's behavior seems to be saying:

_____
_____
_____
_____
_____
_____
_____

☐ This person prepared well.

☐ This person could have prepared better by:

_____
_____

Continued on next page

6. ☺ _____ or ☹ _____

I really like school!

What the person's behavior seems to be saying:

_____

_____

_____

_____

_____

_____

☐ This person prepared well.

☐ This person could have prepared better by:

_____

_____

7. ☺ _____ or ☹ _____

What the person's behavior seems to be saying:

_____

_____

_____

_____

_____

_____

☐ This person prepared well.

☐ This person could have prepared better by:

_____

_____

CHAPTER 7 Applying For a Job

| ACTIVITY 8 | *You're the Boss* |

for use with Lesson 7.2

Your Goal: Evaluate the qualifications of people who are applying for a job.

What to Do: Read the classified ad below. Then read the notes the employer has written about the people who have interviewed for the position. Compare their qualities to the qualifications described in the ad. Then decide which person you would hire.

EXCEPTIONAL SALES POSITION

Sales position available with an industry leader in distribution and manufacturing of quality lines of building materials. Candidate must be self-motivated, aggressive individual. Company automobile provided. We are a growing company in need of people to grow with us. Send detailed résumé in confidence to:

C & D LUMBER SUPPLY
P.O. Box 193
South Windsor, CT 06074

Notes by the employer:

1. *Cindy S.: Good school record. Seems eager to learn. Enthusiastic. No experience with building materials. Excellent recommendations. Held several jobs while in school . . . waiting tables, yardwork, babysitting, sales. Résumé well done.*

2. *John J.: School record fair. Quiet, a little hard to talk with. Building materials experience. Had other jobs . . . landscaping, gas station, lumberyard.*

3. *Peter S.: School record poor, attendance also poor. Outgoing, likeable. Knew about building industry. Could talk easily about it. Other jobs . . . lumberyard, hardware store. Familiar with building "jargon." Résumé handwritten, poorly organized.*

Continued on next page

Critical Thinking

1. Based on the qualifications described in the ad, which person will you select?

_____

_____

_____

_____

2. Why did you select this person?

_____

_____

_____

3. Why did you reject the other people?

Second Choice:

_____

_____

_____

_____

_____

Third Choice:

_____

_____

_____

_____

_____

CHAPTER 8 On the Job

ACTIVITY 1   *From School to Work—A Big Change*
for use with Lesson 8.1

Your Goal: Learn about some of the ways that work is different from school.

What to Do: Pretend that a friend is having a conversation with you about the first week on the job. Think about how work is different from school and how you would respond to your friend. Then answer the questions.

Your Friend's Conversation

"Wow, am I glad to finish this week of work. I didn't believe it would ever end. Why didn't someone tell me what real work was like? I felt embarrassed because I wore the wrong clothes. I wonder if all jobs are like the one I have."

"My boss doesn't know what the word patience means. I feel as if he is staring at me all the time. He has never once told me I'm doing a good job, and I think I'm doing OK. What does he want? After all, it's my first week of work. I know I'm slow, but I'm trying my best. He makes me so nervous that I keep making mistakes."

"One time I forgot what he told me to do. I was really afraid to ask him a question. I thought he might think I was dumb or something. So I just went ahead and did the job. Just my luck, it wasn't right. Boy, did I make a big mistake."

"You know what else gets me? Some of the lazy people I work with. Here are some of us really working, and there they are dragging around not doing their share. We are all getting paid about the same. It's not right. I sure hope it's better next week. I think they are going to give me an orientation. It'll be a little late, but it sure would help."

Your Response to Your Friend

You can help your friend by giving some thoughtful advice. In numbers 1–4, write down what you will say. Identify at least four points which may help your friend at work. Briefly explain each point you make.

1. _____

   _____

Continued on next page

2. _____

_____

_____

3. _____

_____

_____

4. _____

_____

Other points: _____

_____

Critical Thinking

1. School and work have many similarities as well as differences. List below
   the ways you think school and work are similar. For example, you must be
   on time at school and at work.

   _____

   _____

   _____

2. What do you or other students wear to school that you would probably not
   wear on the job?

   _____

   _____

   _____

3. How would you react if your coworkers were being lazy?

   _____

   _____

   _____

   _____

File in your Career Resource File.

CHAPTER 8 On the Job

ACTIVITY 2   *Your Work Hours and Pay*

for use with Lesson 8.1

Your Goal: Read the classified ads in your newspaper to learn about work schedules and the different ways people are paid.

What to Do: Study different types of work schedules and methods of payment you find in the classified ads.

Cut out four classified ads that mention work schedules and four classified ads that mention methods of payment. Attach the ads to this page in the spaces provided below. Then answer the questions.

Examples of Work Schedules

Cut out four ads that describe work schedules and attach them below. Label each ad with the type of work schedule advertised.

1. Work Schedule _____   2. Work Schedule _____   3. Work Schedule _____   4. Work Schedule _____

Critical Thinking

1. Did you find that most of the ads in the newspaper listed the work schedules?

_____

_____

2. Name two schedules listed most frequently.

_____

_____

_____

Continued on next page

Examples of Methods of Payment

Cut out four ads that mention pay and attach them below. Label each ad with the method of payment advertised.

1. Payment Method   **2.** Payment Method   **3.** Payment Method   **4.** Payment Method

_____   _____   _____   _____

Critical Thinking

1. Did most of the ads in the newspaper list the method and amount of payment? Explain.

_____

_____

_____

2. What types of jobs had lower amounts paid? Give some examples.

_____

_____

_____

3. What types of jobs had higher amounts paid? Give some examples.

_____

_____

_____

4. Did any ads mention benefits in addition to pay? Benefits are "extras" that are considered part of your pay. They might include health insurance, paid time off, retirement plans, child care, and education assistance. What benefits were mentioned in any of the ads?

_____

_____

_____

CHAPTER 8 On the Job

ACTIVITY 3 *Key Terms to Use on the Job*

for use with Lesson 8.1

Your Goal: Learn the key terms you will need on the job.

What to Do: Choose the correct key terms from the following list to complete the sentences below. Find the terms in the Word Search Puzzle that follows. Then answer the Critical Thinking questions.

SUPERVISOR   ENTRY-LEVEL   DISCRIMINATE   WAGES

SALARY   COMMISSION   EMPLOYEE   BENEFITS

ORIENTATION   MINIMUM WAGE   COWORKERS   OVERTIME

1. _____ are the people you work with.

2. The _____ is the person who assigns, checks, and evaluates your work.

3. A lower-level full-time job is called an _____ job.

4. _____ are a fixed amount of money paid for each hour worked.

5. _____ is a fixed amount of money paid for a certain period of time, such as a month.

6. _____ are the "extras" an employer provides in addition to pay.

7. If you work on _____, you earn your pay based on how much you sell.

8. The _____ is the lowest hourly wage an employer can pay for a worker's services.

9. To say that an employer cannot _____ against you means you cannot be treated unfairly because of race, age, gender, religion, nationality, physical appearance, or disability.

10. An _____ is someone who works for a person or business for pay.

Continued on next page

11. Some businesses will give an _____ for new employees so that they will understand the company's policies and ways of doing things.

12. When you work more than 40 hours in a week, you are working _____ .

Now find and circle the key terms in the Word Search puzzle below. The terms could be horizontal, vertical, or diagonal. Hint: some terms are written backwards.

```
Q L I H C R N A S Q V M R S A E T P
I S O U T L O N N M T S V R T U S L
I B K W S D I S C R I M I N A T E E
L L V S E M T U O T R J M S T S N V
S S T L K I A P M V N S T R M F T E
A T U V F N T E M C O W O R K E R S
E S R E S I N R I V W T A J A E Y A
T P N Q S M E V S M N Z R G E A L L
V E L E O U I I S T U S E A E T E A
B L S T E M R S I I K J T M E S V R
P B T V E W O O O E E Y O L P M E Y
O C J A R A C R N H I E T U S L L K
M G U M D G S L N K T V V Z Q U T M
E A U A E E M I T R E V O S T R V E
```

Critical Thinking

1. What kinds of information would you give to new students at an orientation meeting for your school? List at least five things you would tell newcomers about your school.

_____

_____

2. Can you name some of the benefits a company might offer to its employees?

_____

_____

3. Create a scene for a soap opera or TV show in which an employer discriminates against an employee. Write a dialogue between the employer and the employee.

_____

_____

_____

File in
your Career
Resource File.

CHAPTER 8 On the Job

ACTIVITY 4   *Interview With an Employer*
for use with Lesson 8.2

Your Goal: Interview an employer to find out what will be expected of you on the job.

What to Do: Locate an employer you would like to talk with. Perhaps you can find someone in the career field in which you are interested. Call or make an appointment to speak to the employer in person. Use the questions that follow. Ask any other questions you think of about the employer's expectations for employees.

Write your notes in the spaces provided below. Then summarize what you learned from the employer.

Employer I Interviewed: _____
                            (Name)

_____
(Title)

_____
(Company)

1. What are the most important things you expect from an employee who works for you?

_____

_____

2. How do you handle an employee who doesn't do a full day's work?

_____

_____

3. How can you tell when an employee is taking initiative on the job?

_____

_____

4. Do employees have opportunities to learn new skills on the job?

_____

_____

Continued on next page

Chapter 8 • Exploring Careers   **97**

5. How important is friendliness and cooperation?

_____

_____

6. How would you describe a dependable worker?

_____

_____

7. How do you evaluate an employee's work? Does your company have performance reviews?

_____

_____

8. What kind of employee orientation does your company have? Are mentors assigned to new employees during orientation?

_____

_____

9. Does your company have a dress code? What is it?

_____

_____

10. How would you describe your company's corporate culture?

_____

_____

_____

Critical Thinking

After your interview with the employer, consider all that was said. Then summarize what you learned. Was there any information that surprised you? Explain.

_____

_____

_____

_____

_____

CHAPTER **8** On the Job

File in your Career Resource File.

ACTIVITY 5	*Evaluation on the Job*

for use with Lesson 8.2

Your Goal: Learn to evaluate your work as a student (or as an employee if you have a job).

What to Do: Following is an evaluation form used for a performance review. Answer as many of the questions as possible by placing a check mark in the box marked Unsatisfactory, Satisfactory, or Excellent.

If you do not have a job, evaluate yourself as a student. If a question does not apply, write N/A (not applicable). Then answer the Critical Thinking questions.

Employee Performance Review			
Factors	**Unsatisfactory**	**Satisfactory**	**Excellent**
Works well with others (Cooperates)			
Follows directions (Understands what to do and does it)			
Takes initiative (Does what needs to be done without being told)			
Takes on responsibility (Accepts a task and finishes it)			
Continues to learn (Willing to learn new things)			
Works by the rules (Behaves ethically and honestly)			
Basic skills Reading			
Writing			
Mathematics			
Speaking			
Listening			
Performance Factors Total			

Continued on next page

Chapter 8 • Exploring Careers   99

Critical Thinking

1. Could you improve any areas on your performance review? What areas could you improve?

_____

_____

_____

_____

_____

_____

_____

_____

2. List and describe three steps you could take to improve in those areas.

_____

_____

_____

_____

_____

_____

_____

_____

_____

_____

_____

CHAPTER 9 Working With Others

ACTIVITY 1   *Seeing Other Points of View*

for use with Lesson 9.1

Your Goal: Practice seeing the other person's viewpoint.

What to Do: In the following exercise, you will read several short scenes. Rewrite the second speaker's response so that it shows an understanding of the first person's point of view.

Example:

> *Zack to his boss:* "I hate doing this job. It's really too hard for me. I don't like lifting all these boxes."
>
> *Boss:* "You had better just do the job and be quiet."

Rewrite the reaction of the boss to show that he understands Zack's point of view:

A possible reaction of the boss that would show that he understands Zack's point of view would be, "I realize that this is really hard work, but it is part of the job and must be done."

Now it's your turn to rewrite the responses.

1. > *Michael to his mother:* "Mom, I want to go to the party on Saturday. There will be lots of kids there from school, and Kim's parents will be there for sure."
   >
   > *Mother:* "No. Definitely not. You're too young to go to parties."

Rewrite the mother's response to show that she understands Michael's point of view:

Mother: _____

_____

_____

_____

_____

_____

_____

_____

Continued on next page

Chapter 9 • Exploring Careers   101

2. *Father to his son, Arsenio:* "I want you to do your chores. The house needs to be cleaned up because we are having people over for dinner tonight."

Arsenio: "I just can't do them right now, Dad. My friend is waiting for me to work on our science project. I'll do them later. 'Bye!"

Rewrite Arsenio's answer to show that he understands his father's point of view.

Arsenio: _____

_____

_____

_____

_____

_____

_____

3. *Teacher to student, Emma:* "You had better get to class on time and get your homework in or you will be failing this class. I'm really worried about you, Emma."

Emma: "I don't care. I don't like this class."

Rewrite Emma's answer to show that she understands her teacher's point of view.

Emma: _____

_____

_____

_____

_____

_____

_____

_____

_____

_____

_____

Critical Thinking

1. Think of your own example of something your parent or guardian said to you that may have caused a disagreement.

   What your parent said: _____

   _____

   _____

   _____

   _____

   Your reaction to your parent's statement: _____

   _____

   _____

   _____

   _____

   Now rewrite your own reaction to show that you recognize your parent's point of view.

   _____

   _____

   _____

   _____

2. Now think of something you have said that wasn't understood or caused a disagreement with someone.

   What you said: _____

   _____

   _____

   _____

   _____

Continued on next page

The other person's reaction: _____

_____

_____

_____

_____

_____

Now rewrite the other person's reaction to show an understanding of your viewpoint.

_____

_____

_____

_____

_____

_____

3. How does it make you feel when someone sees your point of view? Explain in a few sentences.

_____

_____

_____

_____

_____

_____

_____

File in
your Career
Resource File.

CHAPTER 9   Working With Others

ACTIVITY 2   *Handling Criticism*

for use with Lesson 9.1

Your Goal: Learn how to give and receive criticism in a positive way.

What to Do: Write a brief summary of a recent situation in which you were criticized. (If you cannot think of one, imagine a scene in which someone criticizes you for the way you are dressed.)

The Criticism: Describe below how and why you were criticized.

_____

_____

_____

Analyze the way the other person criticized you by answering these questions and explaining your answers.

1. Was the criticism given in a calm or angry voice? Explain.

_____

_____

2. Did the discussion center on the problem or on you? Explain.

_____

_____

3. Were hurtful remarks made? Who made them? Explain.

_____

_____

4. Were suggestions for improvement given? What were the suggestions?

_____

_____

Continued on next page

Handling the Criticism

Now analyze the way you handled the criticism. Answer each question in one or two sentences.

1. Did you blame other people or other things? Whom or what did you blame?

_____

_____

_____

2. Did you admit the problem but try to get the person to feel sorry for you? Explain.

_____

_____

_____

_____

3. Did you get mad at yourself and put yourself down? Explain.

_____

_____

_____

_____

4. Did you get angry about the criticism and stay upset for a long time? What did you do?

_____

_____

_____

_____

5. If you could do it over again, how would you handle the situation? What would you do or say?

_____

_____

_____

_____

CHAPTER 9 Working With Others

File in your Career Resource File.

ACTIVITY 3 *Problem Solving on the Job*

for use with Lesson 9.1

Your Goal: Explore a method of problem solving to use on the job or in personal relationships.

What to Do: Try your hand at phantom or make-believe problem solving. Then, when you have a real problem, you can use the same skills to solve it. Read the following account of Natasha's problem. Follow the steps in conflict resolution to decide how you would handle it. The steps in conflict resolution are explained in your textbook.

Natasha's Problem

Natasha was pleased with her job. It wasn't the first job she had ever had, but it was her first full-time job. She wanted to be successful. She didn't feel she was being paid enough money, but she was learning new skills and was getting more responsibility.

Natasha enjoyed her work. She looked forward to going to work every day. There were some times that she didn't enjoy, however. These times always seemed to involve Allen. Allen had worked at Production Arts longer than she had. He was not her boss, but since he had worked there longer, he seemed to have more authority.

Allen did everything himself. He did not know how to delegate authority. He didn't seem to be able to let other people help him do the work. As a result, at least once a week he got far behind. When he got behind, Natasha got behind too. Her work depended on Allen getting his work done.

Natasha was a good organizer and had a quick mind. She could see some things Allen could do to make his work easier if he would only learn how to delegate jobs to others.

Natasha first needed to get Allen's cooperation in trying to solve the problem. Then Allen and Natasha could work together using the steps in conflict resolution.

Continued on next page

Suggestions for Natasha

Show how they could use those steps to work out the problem.

Step #1: Define the problem

Write out a statement from the point of view of Natasha and then one from the point of view of Allen.

Natasha's statement of the problem: _____

_____

Allen's statement of the problem: _____

_____

Step #2: Suggest a solution

Write out a solution from both points of view—Allen's and Natasha's.

Natasha's solution to the problem: _____

_____

Allen's solution to the problem: _____

_____

Step #3: Evaluate solutions

List the strong and weak points about each solution.

Natasha's solution to the problem:

Strong points: _____

_____

Weak points: _____

_____

Allen's solution to the problem:

Strong points: _____

_____

Weak points: _____

_____

Step #4: Compromise

Try to think of a way to compromise. Someone would have to give up something to come to an agreement. Write out a statement from Natasha and one from Allen.

Natasha's compromise: _____

_____

Allen's compromise: _____

_____

Step #5: Get another point of view

Pretend that you are Natasha's boss and make suggestions for a solution to the problem.

Suggestions for solutions: _____

_____

_____

Critical Thinking

1. Explain why you think your solution to Natasha's problem would work.

_____

_____

_____

_____

_____

2. Apply this five-step process of conflict resolution to one of your own problems. The problem may be with a parent, friend, teacher, brother or sister. Picture the other person in your mind's eye and imagine what the other person would say.

Step #1: Define the problem

What is the conflict? _____

_____

_____

Step #2: Suggest a solution

Your solution: _____

_____

_____

What I think the other person's solution might be: _____

_____

_____

Continued on next page

Step #3: Evaluate solutions

Your solution: _____

_____

_____

What I think the other person's solution might be: _____

_____

_____

Step #4: Compromise

Your compromise: _____

_____

_____

What I think the other person's compromise might be: _____

_____

_____

Step #5: Get another person's point of view
Ask a friend, counselor, or teacher to give you another point of view.

_____

_____

_____

3. Do you think this five-step method would work to help you solve your own
conflicts? Why or why not?

_____

_____

_____

_____

_____

_____

_____

_____

File in
your Career
Resource File.

CHAPTER 9 Working With Others

ACTIVITY 4   *Steps to Successful Teamwork*

for use with Lesson 9.2

Your Goal: Apply the three steps to successful teamwork to a work situation.

What to Do: Read the following description of Walt's work situation. Then analyze the problems by following the steps in team planning: setting goals, assigning tasks, communicating about how things are going.

Walt's Work

Walt was fortunate to get a summer job in the recreation department at the park. He thought the job was a prize because summer jobs were not easy to find.

Everything seemed to be going along nicely the first three weeks. Just about that time things really started to get busy.

Walt's department was trying to plan the dedication of a new recreation center at one of the parks. Walt's boss, Mrs. Tanner, asked everyone to take shorter lunch breaks and work really hard until the dedication ceremony. She thought people would get more work done that way.

Walt wanted this job, but he hadn't expected all this stress. Things just weren't organized. The department members didn't seem to work together as a team. He wasn't sure what he was supposed to do.

On the day of the dedication everything seemed to go out of control. The mayor and other guests were there, along with many guests from the city. Walt's department was supposed to deliver the sound equipment. Walt was responsible for setting up the chairs, but nothing arrived on time. Mrs. Tanner wanted to know what had happened.

One of Walt's coworkers, John, said he put the order in for the sound equipment but that someone in the office must have misplaced the paperwork. Walt thought the chairs would be delivered, but Mrs. Tanner told him he should have ordered them himself. Mrs. Tanner said that this was not the time to make mistakes. They had no sound equipment and no chairs. The whole city would know about it. How would the recreation department look? How would she look? She wanted to fire everyone.

Continued on next page

Analyze the Problem

How could Mrs. Tanner solve the problems in the recreation department? Pretend that you are Mrs. Tanner. Follow the steps that follow for achieving good teamwork.

1. **Set goals:** Describe how Mrs. Tanner and members of her team could set goals. What would the goals be?

_____

_____

2. **Assign roles and tasks:** Did everyone have a role? What could be done to make things run more smoothly?

_____

_____

3. **Assess the progress:** Did they ever discuss the project? What could they have done?

_____

_____

Critical Thinking

1. What could Walt do to create a better working environment?

_____

_____

2. Imagine that you are getting together with a group of friends to plan an event—a dance, party, or a trip to the mall.

   Follow the three steps for working as a team.

   Set goals: Name your goals.

   _____

   _____

   Assign roles and tasks: Assign a job to each friend.

   _____

   _____

   Assess progress: Have you made adequate plans for the event? Could you do anything else?

   _____

   _____

CHAPTER 9 Working With Others

ACTIVITY 5 *Problems Teams Face*

for use with Lesson 9.2

Your Goal: Practice looking at the problems teams face in accomplishing their tasks.

What to Do: Read a scene describing a freshman class meeting. Then match the events during the meeting to a list of typical problems teams face.

The freshman class meets during lunch in room 202 to plan a dance. This is what happens during their meeting:

1. About twenty freshmen arrive for the meeting during lunch.

2. No one knows who is in charge of planning the dance.

3. Some members are just sitting in the back of the room talking to their friends.

4. Then two of the class officers start to argue about how the dance should be planned.

5. The president of the class thinks she is not getting enough recognition for all of her work, so she gets up and leaves.

6. The vice-president tries to get the group to vote on a dance chairperson.

7. Selma says she is the most qualified and starts arguing with Arthur, who says he is the most qualified to do the job.

8. The bell rings, lunch is over, and nothing is accomplished.

Now read the list of typical problems teams face. Next to each write the number of the sentence from the scene above that applies. Hint: Not all of the sentences above will be used and some statements below may have more than one answer.

A. Some team members are competing with others. _____

B. No one is sure who is really in charge. _____

C. The goals of the group are not clear. _____

D. Some team members aren't working as hard as others. _____

E. Some team members feel they are not getting recognized. _____

Continued on next page

Critical Thinking

Have you been a member of a team? Of course you have. Your family is a team. Describe one of the problems in working together as a team that has occurred in your family. Examples would be planning a trip, an outing, a birthday party, or just what to do on Sunday.

_____

_____

_____

_____

_____

_____

_____

_____

_____

_____

_____

_____

_____

_____

_____

_____

_____

_____

_____

_____

_____

_____

CHAPTER 10 Basic Skills Count

ACTIVITY 1   *Listen to Someone Listen*

for use with Lesson 10.1

Your Goal: Analyze the way one person listens to another.

What to Do: Be alert to poor listening habits. Read Dave and Linda's conversation. Look at the list of active listening skills. How would you rate Dave as a listener?

Dave and Linda's Conversation

Dave: Linda, we need to get to work on the tickets for the school dance. Can we meet Wednesday after school? It's a good time for me. I'm busy the rest of the week. (Dave is looking through papers in his backpack as he talks to Linda.)

Linda: It's not the best time for me, but I could change some things and work with you. How long do you think it will take?

Dave: Listen, I have some great ideas to tell you about. I think this can be the best dance yet. Between you and me, we'll really get those ticket sales organized. (Dave waves to a friend, Mike, across the campus.)

Linda: That's great, Dave. I have thought of some things, too. I know. . .

Dave: I bet some of the people your family knows can get us some free printing and stuff like that. Oh hey, Mike, can you shoot a few baskets after school tomorrow? Listen, Linda, I'll see you. (Dave leaves to join Mike to discuss their basketball plans.)

Continued on next page

Signs of an Active Listener

Look at the three points that follow that are signs of being a good listener. Rate Dave as poor, average, or good on each point listed. Then explain why you gave him that rating.

1. How does Dave rate as an active listener? Does he focus on the main ideas that Linda is communicating?

   Dave's rating (Circle one):   Poor   Average   Good

   Explain: _____

   _____

   _____

   _____

   _____

2. Does he use positive body language and facial expressions to respond?

   Dave's rating (Circle one):   Poor   Average   Good

   Explain: _____

   _____

   _____

   _____

   _____

3. Does he react by making comments and asking questions?

   Dave's rating (Circle one):   Poor   Average   Good

   Explain: _____

   _____

   _____

   _____

   _____

CHAPTER 10 Basic Skills Count

ACTIVITY 2 *Cluttered Messages*
for use with Lesson 10.1

Your Goal: Learn to recognize and correct cluttered messages.

What to Do: Following are some business memos that are cluttered with too many words. Figure out what the message is. Then rewrite the sentences to make the point clearer.

Sentence Rewrites

1. This is in reference to your letter of 10 December in which you requested further information about whether your order had been received, and you also asked whether you needed to furnish additional descriptions of what you wanted.

   Your Rewrite:

   _____

   _____

   _____

   _____

   _____

2. We realize that any failure during one or more of the steps we have to take could possibly result in our failure to meet the deadline we all had agreed upon when we met together the last time we had our annual meeting.

   Your Rewrite:

   _____

   _____

   _____

   _____

   _____

   _____

Continued on next page

3. Unless we make every attempt to look into the many, many, possibly twenty or so, problems we face, we will never be able to complete this project because the costs will continue to increase and get higher.

Your Rewrite:

_____

_____

_____

_____

_____

4. Company health records are further broken down into two sections which are medical records and dental records. Medical records appear on form 10-A and the dental records appear on form 10-B.

Your Rewrite:

_____

_____

_____

_____

_____

5. This decision states that the company will do everything that a company can do to help employees to be happy employees and to do their best work for our company and to be productive so that our company can continue to grow and become larger.

Your Rewrite:

_____

_____

_____

_____

_____

_____

Date Assigned   **Date Completed**

CHAPTER 10 Basic Skills Count

File in your Career Resource File.

ACTIVITY 3   *Communication Is a Two-Step Process*

for use with Lesson 10.1

Your Goal: Practice writing a memo or e-mail message.

What to Do: Use the following six words in a paragraph. The paragraph should be no longer than six sentences. Assume you are writing a memo or E-mail message to employees in your company. Then test your written message using the checklist that begins on the following page.

The words to use: advertise   customers   product
sales   message   competition

Your Message

_____

_____

_____

_____

_____

_____

_____

_____

_____

_____

_____

_____

_____

_____

_____

Continued on next page

Check Your Message

How well did you do? Put your message through the following test.

1. What was your most important point?

_____

_____

_____

2. Give your message to someone else to read. Did the person understand what you were trying to say? Explain.

_____

_____

_____

3. Evaluate your message. Check Yes or No after each answer.

Did you state your most important point first?　☐ **Yes**　☐ **No**

Was the message brief? Did it stick to the point?　☐ **Yes**　☐ **No**

Was the writing clear?　☐ **Yes**　☐ **No**

Explain: _____

_____

_____

Was the writing accurate (spelling, grammar, and punctuation)?　☐ **Yes**　☐ **No**

Explain: _____

_____

_____

4. Based on this review, rewrite your message as necessary.

_____

_____

_____

_____

_____

_____

CHAPTER 10 Basic Skills Count

ACTIVITY 4 *Words in Context*

for use with Lesson 10.1

Your Goal: Try using context clues to understand the words that may be unfamiliar to you.

What to Do: In the sentences that follow, write the meaning you think the word has in context. Then compare your definition to the one in the dictionary. If they are different, write the definition from the dictionary.

1. The *brevity* of his remarks let everyone know that he was in a hurry.

   Brevity means _____

   _____

2. He had a hard time *coping* with his problems.

   Coping means _____

   _____

3. The company *defaulted* on their payments and had to go out of business.

   Defaulted means _____

   _____

4. He had high *expectations* for his success since he was so well qualified for the job.

   Expectations means _____

   _____

5. She *fostered* good relations with employees by being polite and courteous.

   Fostered means _____

   _____

6. John asked Ginger to *generate* as many ideas as she could think of.

   Generate means _____

   _____

Continued on next page

Chapter 10 • Exploring Careers 121

7. His *justification* for firing the employee was that the employee stole money from the company.

Justification means _____

_____

8. Her boss asked her to have the picture *laminated* to protect it.

Laminated means _____

_____

9. The president thought the company would reach *optimum* conditions for growth next year.

Optimum means _____

_____

10. The problems could not be *resolved* until each coworker considered the other person's viewpoint.

Resolved means _____

_____

11. *Stagnant* business conditions caused the company's losses in the last quarter.

Stagnant means _____

_____

12. Because there was very little interest in the program, it was *terminated*.

Terminated means _____

_____

13. Ms. Ragza thought the style had *universal* appeal and would do well in the marketplace.

Universal means _____

_____

14. Her boss asked her to *verify* the facts by checking the records.

Verify means _____

_____

15. He read the *warranty* to be sure it covered the points he thought were important.

Warranty means _____

_____

CHAPTER 10 Basic Skills Count

ACTIVITY 5   *Use Your Math*
for use with Lesson 10.2

Your Goal: Practice using your math skills in situations you may encounter in your daily life.

What to Do: Sharpen your pencil. Try your hand at some math problems you might encounter. Use the space provided for figuring and for your answers.

1. The Office Party

One of your friends at the office is celebrating his birthday next week. You are organizing the office party. Fifteen people have contributed $4.00 each for a small gift and refreshments. You are in charge of deciding how the money will be spent. How much will you spend on a gift, and how much will you spend on refreshments?

Estimate how much you would spend on the gift. Then use the following grocery store prices to decide on the refreshments you can serve. Do not go over the total amount of money you collected.

Grocery Items	
soft drinks	$ .50 each
potato chips	$ 1.89 for 16 oz. bag which serves 8
cookies	$ 2.89 for 2 dozen cookies
crackers	$ 2.69 for snack-type crackers for dips
cheese dip	$ 1.59 for 8 oz. which serves 8
sheet cake	$20.00 serves 20 people

Continued on next page

Figure it out:

Total people attending party:		
Total collected:		
Total for food:	soft drinks	_____
	potato chips	_____
	cookies	_____
	crackers	_____
	cheese dip	_____
	sheet cake	_____
		Total:
Cost of gift:		
Total Spent:		

2. Stocking up on Your Wardrobe

You need some new clothes. After looking over your clothes and comparison shopping, you decide you want to purchase the following clothes at the prices listed. You earn $100.00 a week. You can save all of your earnings except $20.00 a week for lunches and bus fare. How long would it take you to save for these clothes? Remember—include the cost of sales tax if your state has one. If you do not know what it is in your state, pretend that it is 5 percent.

Clothes You Plan to Buy

one heavy jacket	$50.00
two pairs of jeans	$25.00 each
three shirts	$20.00 each
one pair athletic shoes	$60.00
six pairs socks	$ 3.00 a pair

Figure it out:

How much you make each week:	
How much you save each week:	
Cost of clothes:	_____
Tax:	_____
Total cost of clothes:	
How many weeks it will take to save for clothes:	

3. Best Buys

You need to buy toothpaste, deodorant, and suntan lotion. You are interested in getting the best buy for your money. While shopping in the store you have narrowed your choice down to the following. Which will you buy?

Toothpaste

Figure it out:

Smiles	6 oz.	$1.29	How much per ounce? _____
Tartar Free	12 oz.	$2.49	How much per ounce? _____
Bright	16 oz.	$3.19	How much per ounce?
Which one will you buy?			

Sunscreen Lotion

Bronze Smart	16 oz.	$3.78	How much per ounce? _____
Ray Block	24 oz.	$6.00	How much per ounce? _____
Healthy Glow	8 oz.	$2.98	How much per ounce?
Which one will you buy?			

Deodorant

Fresh	8 oz.	$2.39	How much per ounce? _____
Clean Scent	10 oz.	$2.59	How much per ounce? _____
Spring	12 oz.	$2.98	How much per ounce?
Which one will you buy?			

Continued on next page

4. The Gift Coupon

You have won a $20.00 gift coupon at Famous Foods restaurant. You have invited two friends to help you spend it. You can't spend over the twenty dollar amount. What will you order? The following foods are on the menu. Pretend that there is a 7 percent state tax on the food eaten out.

Menu   **Figure it out:**

Superburger	$3.29	Food to order _____
Hamburger	2.39	_____
Veggieburger	2.59	_____
French Fries	1.59	_____
Soft Drink	.99	_____
Milk	.99	_____

Cost of food for three people: _____

7% Tax: _____

Total cost: _____

5. The Scheduler

It's your job to schedule people to answer the phone for a charity telethon. The phones are being answered during the following times:

Monday, Tuesday, Wednesday   8 A.M.–6 P.M.
Thursday, Friday   8 A.M.–9 P.M.
Saturday   8 A.M.–5 P.M.

You need four people to cover the phones at all times. You already have two full-time people who will work 40 hours during the week. How many part-time people do you need who will work 20 hours each?

Figure it out:

Your answer:

CHAPTER 11 Staying Healthy and Safe

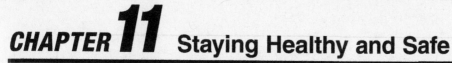

ACTIVITY 1 *Good Advice*

for use with Lesson 11.1

Your Goal: Give yourself some good healthy advice.

What to Do: Read the letter sent by "Miserable and Alone" to an advice columnist. Then play the role of the advice columnist and try to help Miserable and Alone overcome the problem.

Dear Answer Person,

I really have a problem. I can't stop eating. Pizza, potato chips, cookies, ice cream--anything I can find. At night I hide in my room, watch TV and eat. That's all I want to do. I'm too embarrassed to ride my bike or get any exercise because I'm so overweight. Please help me stop overeating.

Sincerely,
Miserable and Alone

Your response as the Answer Person: _____

_____

_____

_____

_____

_____

_____

_____

Continued on next page

Chapter 11 • Exploring Careers 127

Now write a letter to the Answer Person asking advice about your *own* worst health habit. It may be that you don't eat enough fruits and vegetables, or you don't get enough exercise.

Dear Answer Person,

_____

_____

_____

_____

_____

_____

Sincerely,

_____
(Your Name)

Again, take the role of the Answer Person and respond to your own letter.

Dear _____ **,**
      (Your Name)

_____

_____

_____

_____

_____

_____

_____

Sincerely,
Answer Person

File in your Career Resource File.

CHAPTER 11 Staying Healthy and Safe

ACTIVITY 2 *Reducing Stress*

for use with Lesson 11.1

Your Goal: Analyze how you react to stress and how you can reduce the stress in your life.

What to Do: In the activity below, test your stress quotient to help you relax and get along better with yourself. Check Yes or No next to each statement.

Your Stress Quotient

Yes	No	
☐	☐	**1.** I feel I need to be perfect in most things I do.
☐	☐	**2.** It is important to me that others like me.
☐	☐	**3.** I find it difficult to express my feelings.
☐	☐	**4.** It's important for me to win.
☐	☐	**5.** I eat when I'm nervous.
☐	☐	**6.** Changes involving school, work, or family make me uneasy.
☐	☐	**7.** I often feel tired and run-down.
☐	☐	**8.** I feel myself rushing through the day.
☐	☐	**9.** I am often late for things.

Your Score

The more "yes" answers you checked above, the higher your stress quotient. What can you do to handle the stress in your life? Read the following suggestions. Decide which ones would help you. Check "yes" or "no" next to each suggestion.

Yes	No	
☐	☐	**1.** Realize I don't need to be perfect in everything I do.
☐	☐	**2.** Learn how to tell people the way I feel.
☐	☐	**3.** Begin to set some goals and prioritize them (put them in order of importance).
☐	☐	**4.** Allow some time for unexpected things that happen.
☐	☐	**5.** Take some time to relax—daydream, get lost in a book, in a film, or in music.

Continued on next page

Critical Thinking

1. Make a list of at least three things that happen that cause stress in your life.

_____

_____

_____

_____

_____

_____

_____

_____

2. Now write down three things you can do to relieve each of those three stresses.

_____

_____

_____

_____

_____

_____

_____

_____

_____

_____

_____

_____

CHAPTER **11** Staying Healthy and Safe

ACTIVITY 3   *Health and Safety Awareness*

for use with Lesson 11.2

Your Goal: Create advertising campaigns to promote health and safety.

What to Do: You are going to plan two public service advertising promotions. The first one is an anti-drug campaign. As part of your campaign, you will be designing a T-shirt, a bumper sticker, a billboard, and a lapel button. Write your slogans on the sketches below and decorate each sketch to show off your designs.

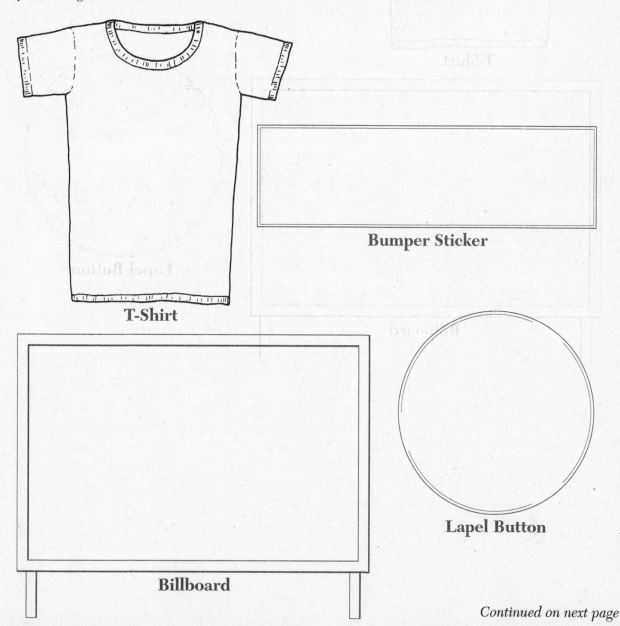

T-Shirt

Bumper Sticker

Lapel Button

Billboard

Continued on next page

Now imagine that you are planning a campaign to promote safety in the workplace. Once again, you will be designing a T-shirt, a bumper sticker, a billboard, and a lapel button. Write your slogans on the sketches below, and decorate each sketch to show off your designs.

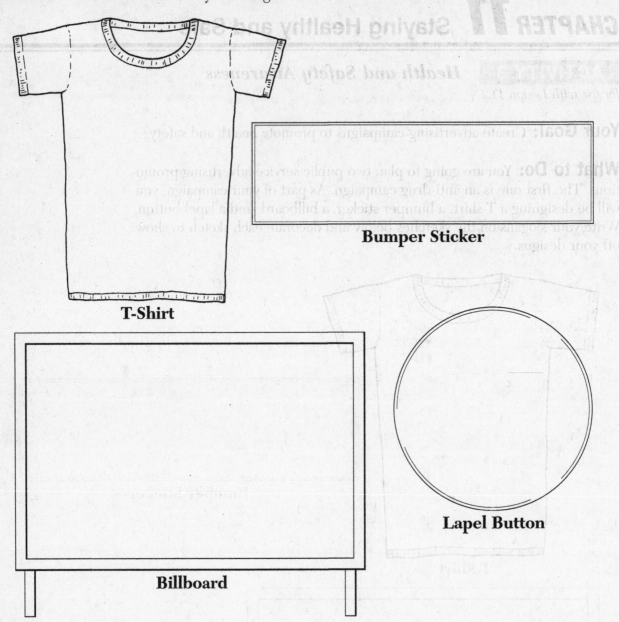

T-Shirt

Bumper Sticker

Lapel Button

Billboard

CHAPTER  Staying Healthy and Safe

ACTIVITY 4   *Safety Checklist*
for use with Lesson 11.2

Your Goal: Inspect your home for its safety features.

What to Do: Put a check next to each statement that describes you or your home. Then answer the questions that follow.

☐ All chemicals and cleaners are clearly marked and kept out of the reach of any children.

☐ All unused poisonous substances are disposed of in the proper way.

☐ The stairs and hallways in my home are kept clear and well-lighted.

☐ All rugs in my home are nonskid rugs.

☐ All the electrical wires in my home are in good condition.

☐ I discard medicines that have reached their expiration date.

☐ I use electrical appliances according to the manufacturers' directions.

☐ A fire extinguisher is kept in a convenient place in my home.

☐ Flammable materials are stored properly in my home.

☐ My home has working smoke detectors.

☐ My family has established an escape plan in case of fire or other emergency.

☐ Basic first aid equipment—including bandages, ointment for cuts and burns, and antiseptic cleanser—is kept in my home.

Continued on next page

Critical Thinking

1. What other steps could you or your family take to make your home a safer place? Look around your home and yard to see if you can find any other conditions that might be unsafe. List them below. Then tell what you or your family members could do to correct the problems.

Unsafe condition	How to correct the condition
_____	_____
_____	_____
_____	_____
_____	_____
_____	_____
_____	_____

2. Do you think that most accidents in the home could be prevented with a little planning? Why or why not?

_____

_____

_____

_____

_____

_____

3. Do you think the safety planning steps used to prevent accidents at home would also prevent accidents in the workplace?

_____

_____

_____

_____

_____

_____

_____

CHAPTER 12 Moving Toward Your Goals

File in your Career Resource File.

ACTIVITY 1 *Attitude Adds Up*

for use with Lesson 12.1

Your Goal: Assess your own attitude.

What to Do: Answer this attitude check as honestly as you can. Read each statement and circle only the numbers that apply to you. Tally your total points at the end.

Points

+5   if you enjoy your life most of the time

+5   if you make some time for yourself each day

+5   if you try to see the positive in negative events

−5   if you emphasize the negative parts of life and the future

−5   if you often say "if only," "but," or "can't"

+5   if you are an active member of an organization or group

+5   if you can enjoy change

−5   if you want things to stay the same

+5   if you are willing to take a chance or risk

−5   if you often put off what needs to be done

Points

+5   if you look for the best in others

+5   if you enjoy being alone with yourself

+5   if you like yourself most of the time

+5   if you stand up for what you believe in and say so

+5   if you have thought of some alternatives or different paths for yourself in the future

−5   if you often remain silent about issues that are important to you

+5   if you are in good overall physical condition

+5   if you are able to handle the problems you face

+5   if you share your talents and abilities with others

+5   if you have done something nice for someone else today

Your Total Points:_____

Continued on next page

What Do Your Points Mean?

75 points: You are positive and can manage life very well.

60–70 points: You are positive most of the time and can handle life well.

45–55 points: You are sometimes positive and may want to work on being a little more positive.

30–40 points: Once in a while you are positive, but you may want to try to change the areas in which you are negative.

0–25 points: You are seldom positive. Are you "happier being unhappy?" Think about it.

Critical Thinking

How did you score on the attitude scale? Most people can improve their attitude in some areas.

List below three ways you can improve your attitude.

_____

_____

_____

_____

_____

_____

_____

_____

_____

_____

_____

_____

_____

_____

_____

CHAPTER 12 Moving Toward Your Goals

ACTIVITY 2 — *Qualities That Lead to Promotions*
for use with Lesson 12.1

Your Goal: Analyze what qualities are most important in getting a promotion on the job.

What to Do: Below are listed the qualities of people who get promoted to higher positions at work. Prioritize the list according to what you think are the most important qualities people need to get promoted.

Number the qualities from 1–10 in order of importance, with #1 being most important.

Qualities

Seniority
  (length of time on the job)

Knowledge and ability to perform
  basic skills

Willingness to learn

Initiative
  (taking the first step)

Perseverance
  (ability to finish what you start)

Cooperativeness

Thinking skills

Adaptability

Education and training

Attitude

Order of Importance

_____

_____

_____

_____

_____

_____

_____

_____

_____

_____

Continued on next page

Critical Thinking

1. Which quality did you choose to be the most important for someone to be promoted to a higher level? Why?

_____

_____

_____

_____

_____

2. Which quality did you choose to be the least important? Why?

_____

_____

_____

_____

_____

_____

3. Compare your list to other students' lists. Do you agree with the rankings on their lists? Why or why not?

_____

_____

_____

_____

_____

_____

_____

_____

CHAPTER **12** Moving Toward Your Goals

Who Is Growing on the Job?

for use with Lesson 12.1

Your Goal: Compare the job performances of two people to decide who is growing on the job.

What to Do: Andy and Gerald work for the same company. Read about their job performances. Then answer the questions.

Andy's Time on the Job

Andy's summer job was helping to unload trucks at the shipping dock. After Andy learned the routine, the job became boring. So he decided that he would become the most efficient truck unloader the company ever employed.

To make his job interesting, Andy tried to think of new ways he could unload the trucks faster, stack the boxes more neatly, and be sure there was no damage to the boxes he unloaded. Andy became quite good. As the weeks passed, he continued to beat his own records for speed, neatness, and safety. He was proud of what he could do.

One day Pete, a full-time employee who worked all year, was out sick. Pete usually took care of checking the shipments to be sure everything was accounted for. Andy asked Mack, his boss, if he could check the shipment out. Mack was happy to have the help and said yes. Andy didn't have any trouble checking out the shipment because he had watched Pete do it every day. Mack was pleased with the way Andy handled the new task.

Before Andy left the job to return to school, he spoke to Mack. Andy said he wondered if next summer he could get a job with more of a challenge. Mack said that might be hard to do for summer work, but he'd look into it. He said he also had some contacts in town and would put in a good word if Andy wanted to work elsewhere.

Continued on next page

Chapter 12 • Exploring Careers 139

Gerald's Time on the Job

Gerald worked in the office. He got the same pay Andy did, and he even got to work in an air-conditioned office during the hot summer months.

He filled in for people who were on vacation or worked for those who needed extra help. Gerald had a variety of things to do. He filed. In fact he did a lot of filing, more than he really wanted to do. He ran errands. Sometimes he answered the telephone. He even used his "hunt and peck" system of typing, which needed a lot of improvement.

Sometimes there wasn't enough work to keep him busy for the whole day. Gerald didn't want to lose the job, so he stretched out whatever he had to do so it would last longer. For example, he would make a lot of typing mistakes and then retype the order five times. He had all kinds of games he played to take up time. Gerald didn't see a lot of future in his job. He was just glad to pick up his paycheck every week.

Critical Thinking

1. Which employee shows more growth on the job?

_____

2. What did this employee do that shows he is using the job to grow?

_____

_____

3. What did the other employee do that shows he isn't growing on the job?

_____

_____

4. What suggestions do you have for the employee who isn't growing on the job?

_____

_____

_____

5. What predictions can you make about the future success of Andy and Gerald?

_____

_____

_____

CHAPTER 12 Moving Toward Your Goals

File in your Career Resource File.

ACTIVITY 4 *Changing Jobs*
for use with Lesson 12.2

Your Goal: Practice reevaluating your goals by networking and by finding out about transfer opportunities within a company.

What to Do: Imagine you are working in your first full-time job. You are ready to move on to another, more challenging job. Imagine how you would do this by using networking or transferring within a company.

Your First Full-time Job

1. Describe the first full-time job you think you will have. Tell what you think your duties will be. Also, explain what you have accomplished in three years in this job.

_____

_____

_____

_____

_____

_____

_____

2. Why do you want to change positions?

_____

_____

_____

_____

_____

_____

Continued on next page

Networking

You are talking to a friend about trying to find another job. Write what you are saying to this friend as you "network."

_____

_____

_____

_____

_____

_____

_____

_____

Transferring Within the Company

You want to find out about job possibilities within the company you presently work for. Write what you are saying to your boss or some other responsible person in the company.

_____

_____

_____

_____

_____

_____

_____

_____

_____

_____

_____

CHAPTER 12 Moving Toward Your Goals

| ACTIVITY 5 | *Leaving a Job* |

for use with Lesson 12.2

Your Goal: Learn the proper way to leave a job.

What to Do: Read about how Jessica went about leaving her job and answer the questions that follow.

Jessica's New Job

Jessica worked for four years as a nurse for Memorial Hospital. She enjoyed the work because she liked to help people. Jessica received very good job evaluations and several increases in salary.

Even though she enjoyed her job, Jessica had given a lot of thought to leaving her position. She knew she wanted to have the time to go back to school and take more classwork. She wasn't exactly sure what she wanted to do. Perhaps she would become a nursing administrator, or teach, or even operate her own nursing service. Because her present work schedule was so demanding, she didn't have the time to take any classes that would help her achieve any of those goals.

Jessica asked several friends about possible job openings. She also registered with a placement service for health-care specialists. Through one of her friends she learned about a job with a private nursing service. The hours would be more flexible, and there would be no weekend shifts to work. The salary would be about the same. The service offered her the job and she accepted.

Jessica then spoke to her supervisor, Ms. Jenkins, giving her two weeks' notice about changing jobs. Ms. Jenkins was sorry to hear about Jessica's plans. She appreciated, however, that Jessica had given her time to get a replacement. She asked Jessica to write a letter of resignation, which would be put into her employment file.

Jessica did not know what to say to the people she worked with. She finally decided not to say anything at all. One day before she left, one of her coworkers said he heard that Jessica was leaving. Jessica told him she was taking another position and that she would miss working at the hospital. Her coworker said that he had wished Jessica had said something about leaving.

Continued on next page

Critical Thinking

1. Do you agree with the way Jessica handled leaving her job at Memorial Hospital?

_____

_____

_____

_____

2. What did Jessica do that you would have done?

_____

_____

_____

3. What did Jessica do that you would not do?

_____

_____

_____

4. Write out a letter of resignation that Jessica might have written.

_____

_____

_____

_____

_____

_____

_____

_____

_____

_____

_____

CHAPTER 13 Our Economic System

File in your Career Resource File.

ACTIVITY 1   *Goods and Services*

for use with Lesson 13.1

Your Goal: Compare the goods and services you use now to those you will need as a working adult.

What to Do: In the space provided, list the five goods and five services that are most important to you right now. Then think about what will be most important to you when you are an adult working full-time.

IMPORTANT TO ME NOW

Goods   **Why This Is Important to Me Now**

1. _____   _____
2. _____   _____
3. _____   _____
4. _____   _____
5. _____   _____

Services   **Why This Is Important to Me Now**

1. _____   _____
2. _____   _____
3. _____   _____
4. _____   _____
5. _____   _____

IMPORTANT TO ME AS AN ADULT

Goods   **Why This Is Important to Me as an Adult**

1. _____   _____
2. _____   _____
3. _____   _____
4. _____   _____
5. _____   _____

Continued on next page

Services	Why This Is Important to Me as an Adult
1. _____	_____
2. _____	_____
3. _____	_____
4. _____	_____
5. _____	_____

Critical Thinking

Think about the goods and services you selected. As a working adult, will you need different goods and services from those you need now as a student? Explain.

_____

_____

_____

_____

_____

_____

_____

_____

_____

_____

_____

_____

_____

_____

_____

_____

_____

_____

_____

_____

CHAPTER 13 Our Economic System

ACTIVITY 2   *How Are Prices Established?*

for use with Lesson 13.1

Your Goal: Learn about how a business owner decides what to charge for goods and services.

What to Do: Interview the manager or the owner of a business that provides goods or services. Ask how prices are set. You can use the following questions.

The person I interviewed: _____

Name of business: _____

Goods or services provided by business: _____

Questions About Pricing

1. What are the factors that determine the price you charge?

_____

_____

_____

2. Which factors do you think are most important?

_____

_____

_____

3. How does your competition influence the price you charge?

_____

_____

_____

4. How do you use pricing to attract customers?

_____

_____

_____

Continued on next page

5. Please explain your most successful pricing decision. Why was it so successful?

_____

_____

6. Can you describe your least successful decision? Why was it unsuccessful?

_____

_____

7. What advice would you give to someone who is going to set prices for the first time?

_____

_____

Other questions I want to ask:

_____

_____

_____

_____

Critical Thinking

Summarize what you have learned about pricing. Write a paragraph explaining how pricing can affect a business.

_____

_____

_____

_____

_____

_____

_____

_____

_____

CHAPTER **13** Our Economic System

| ACTIVITY 3 | *The Economy* |

for use with Lesson 13.1

Your Goal: Analyze a current news article on the economy.

What to Do: Find an article on the economy in a magazine or newspaper. Summarize the article in the space provided below. Then answer the questions about the article.

Hint: Look in the business sections of magazines and newspapers to find your article.

Article About the Economy

Source: _____ **Title of Article:** _____

Summary:

_____

_____

_____

_____

_____

_____

_____

_____

_____

_____

_____

_____

_____

_____

_____

_____

_____

Continued on next page

Economic Terms in the Article on the Economy

Choose one economic term or concept from your article. Define it and explain what is said about it. Example: The article might include the term *consumer*. The article might state that *consumers* will be paying more money for cars this year.

Key term or concept that is covered in my article: _____

What the article says about the key term or concept:

_____

_____

_____

_____

_____

Critical Thinking

1. How does the condition of the economy, as described in the article, affect you and your family?

_____

_____

_____

_____

_____

2. How can the information in the article help you make choices and decisions about a career?

_____

_____

_____

_____

_____

CHAPTER **13** Our Economic System

File in your Career Resource File.

ACTIVITY 4 *The Entrepreneur*

for use with Lesson 13.2

Your Goal: Find out what qualities are needed to become an entrepreneur.

What to Do: Interview an entrepreneur. Use the following questions.

Questions for the Entrepreneur

1. Please describe your business to me.

_____

_____

_____

2. Why did you decide to go into business for yourself?

_____

_____

_____

3. What is your greatest satisfaction?

_____

_____

_____

4. What are some of the problems you face?

_____

_____

_____

5. What kind of person does it take to be an entrepreneur?

_____

_____

_____

Continued on next page

6. What advice would you give to people who want to go into business for themselves?

_____

_____

_____

7. What can I do now to prepare to be an entrepreneur?

_____

_____

_____

Other questions I want to ask:

_____

_____

_____

Critical Thinking

Summarize what you have learned about being an entrepreneur. Write a paragraph describing what you would have to do to become an entrepreneur.

_____

_____

_____

_____

_____

_____

_____

_____

_____

_____

_____

_____

CHAPTER 13 Our Economic System

File in your Career Resource File.

ACTIVITY 5
Small Businesses in Your Community

for use with Lesson 13.2

Your Goal: Become aware of the functions of small businesses in your community.

What to Do: Take a tour through your community to look at the small businesses. Use this form to record your observations about the types of small businesses in your community.

1. Business Name _____

Business Address _____

What need does this business fill in your community?

_____

_____

What specific industry skills does this business owner need to be successful?

_____

_____

Do you think you would enjoy owning a business like this? Explain.

_____

_____

2. Business Name _____

Business Address _____

What need does this business fill in your community?

_____

_____

What specific industry skills does this business owner need to be successful?

_____

_____

Continued on next page

Do you think you would enjoy owning a business like this? Explain.

_____

_____

3. Business Name _____

Business Address _____

What need does this business fill in your community?

_____

_____

What specific industry skills does this business owner need to be successful?

_____

_____

Do you think you would enjoy owning a business like this? Explain.

_____

_____

4. Business Name _____

Business Address _____

What need does this business fill in your community?

_____

_____

What specific industry skills does this business owner need to be successful?

_____

_____

Do you think you would enjoy owning a business like this? Explain.

_____

_____

CHAPTER 13 Our Economic System

File in your Career Resource File.

ACTIVITY 6 *Your Small Business*

for use with Lesson 13.2

Your Goal: Use your hobbies and interests to decide on what kind of small business you might like to have.

What to Do: On the lines below, write your favorite hobbies or interests. Choose one of these and name a small business that you might open that would relate to your hobby or interest. Then answer the Critical Thinking questions.

   Hint: Refer back to the activities in Chapter 1 for your list of hobbies and interests.

My Hobbies and Interests
List your hobbies and interests.

_____

_____

_____

_____

_____

_____

Small business that I might start that relates to one of my hobbies or interests:

_____

_____

_____

_____

_____

_____

Continued on next page

Critical Thinking

1. What type of skills would you need to be successful at this business?

_____

_____

_____

_____

2. Would this be an expensive business to start? Why or why not?

_____

_____

_____

_____

3. Do you think there is a real need for this type of business? Why or why not?

_____

_____

_____

_____

_____

4. Do you think you would enjoy owning and running this type of business? Explain.

_____

_____

_____

_____

_____

_____

File in
your Career
Resource File.

CHAPTER 14 Managing Your Money

| ACTIVITY 1 | *Working Out a Spending Plan* |

for use with Lesson 14.1

Your Goal: Analyze a spending plan.

What to Do: Read the information given below about Juan and his spending plan. Answer the questions about Juan's money-managing skill.

Juan's Spending Plan

Juan works in a grocery store and earns $75 a week take-home pay. Juan's long-term goal is to save one-quarter of the cost of a computer. When he does this, his grandmother has promised to give him one-quarter of the cost and his parents will give him half of the total cost. His short-term goal is to cover his weekly expenses including lunch, school supplies, and bus fare.

This is Juan's spending plan for a typical week during the school year.

SPENDING PLAN

From _____ 3-9 _____ To _____ 3-15 _____

INCOME Source		Estimated Amount	Actual Amount
grocery store paycheck		$ 75.00	$ 75.00
	Total		$ 75.00

FIXED EXPENSES	Amount Set Aside	Actual Amount
School lunches	$ 10.00	$ 10.00
School supplies	$ 5.00	$ 5.00
Bus fare	$ 10.00	$ 10.00

FLEXIBLE EXPENSES		
Clothes	$ 5.00	$ 10.00
Entertainment	$ 5.00	$ 25.00

Total spent	$ 60.00
Total Income	$ 75.00
minus Total Expenses	$ 60.00
Savings	$ 15.00

Continued on next page

Critical Thinking

1. Do you think Juan is doing a good job of managing his money? Why or why not?

_____

_____

_____

2. What advice would you give to Juan about handling his money? Be specific. Keep Juan's long- and short-term goals in mind.

_____

_____

_____

_____

3. Juan's other long-term goal is to finance his college education. Besides starting a savings plan, what other options does Juan have for financing his future education? Suggest a finance method he could use.

_____

_____

_____

_____

_____

4. Refer back to the future education and training needs you noted for yourself in Activity 1 in Chapter 5. Describe the educational finance method you might use to help you pay for this education. Explain why it's a good option for you.

_____

_____

_____

_____

_____

Date Assigned   Date Completed

CHAPTER 14 Managing Your Money

ACTIVITY 2   *Compare Before You Buy*

for use with Lesson 14.2

Your Goal: Learn how to do comparison shopping.

What to Do: Below is a chart that Juan is using to compare computers before he buys one. Read through Juan's notes. Recommend which computer he should buy. Then use the blank chart on the next page to compare a product you will buy (now or in the future).

I am shopping for a _personal computer_

COMPARISONS	PRODUCT A	PRODUCT B
Brand name	Maxdata	Tech Senior
Manufacturer	Basset	Tech Mart
Store selling it	Base House	Computer Whiz
Price	$ 1,000.00	$1,100.00 on sale
If sale price, how long does sale price last?	not on sale	until end of month
Special features	-free word-processing software -free games	-coupon for discount on monitor -free encyclopedia
Store provides service after sale? (Describe)	Yes. Technician works there full-time	None
Warranty (Describe)	90 days	60 days
Recommendations	Sam bought one—likes it	Jean likes hers—says she'd like more programs to run on it

Continued on next page

Suggestions for Juan

Juan should buy the _____

Explain your answer: _____

_____

_____

Now use the chart below to do your own comparison shopping:

I am shopping for a _____		
COMPARISONS	PRODUCT A	PRODUCT B
Brand name		
Manufacturer		
Store selling it		
Price		
If sale price, how long does sale price last?		
Special features		
Store provides service after sale? (Describe)		
Warranty (Describe)		
Recommendations		

I should buy the _____

Reasons for your choice: _____

_____

_____

CHAPTER **14** Managing Your Money

ACTIVITY 3	*Balancing a Check Register*

for use with Lesson 14.2

Your Goal: Learn how to balance a check register.

What to Do: Below are the transactions in a checking account. Use the check register to enter the transactions and balance the register.

Hint: A withdrawal refers to money that you are taking out of your checking account to pay for something. A deposit is money you are putting into your checking account.

Balance Forward 3/10 $95.00

Withdrawals

Date	Check Number	Pay to	For	Amount
3/11	156	Shirt Shop	Shirt	$13.95
3/14	157	Music Store	CDs	$22.93
3/19	158	Cycle Shop	Deposit	$75.00
3/23	159	Gift Shop	Gift	$22.75

Deposits

3/15	$32.00
3/21	$30.00

Bank Charges

3/22	**Service Charge**	$ 2.00

20--		BE SURE TO DEDUCT ANY PER ITEM CHARGES, SERVICE CHARGES, OR FEES THAT MAY APPLY.					
DATE	NUMBER	TRANSACTION DESCRIPTION	(+OR-) OTHER	✓ T	(+) AMOUNT OF DEPOSIT	(−) AMOUNT OF PAYMENT OR WITHDRAWAL	BALANCE FORWARD
		REMEMBER TO RECORD ALL DEPOSITS AND WITHDRAWALS AS WELL AS PRE-AUTHORIZED TRANSACTIONS.					

Continued on next page

Chapter 14 • Exploring Careers

Critical Thinking

1. What is the benefit of keeping an accurate daily balance in your checking account?

_____

_____

_____

_____

_____

_____

_____

2. What do you think would happen if you wrote checks for more than the amount of money you have in your checking account?

_____

_____

_____

_____

_____

_____

CHAPTER 14 Managing Your Money

ACTIVITY 4   *Understanding Sales Credit*

for use with Lesson 14.2

Your Goal: Learn how to read a credit statement.

What to Do: Below is a monthly statement for sales credit. Look over the statement and answer the questions that follow.

PLEASE DETACH AND RETURN TOP PORTION WITH YOUR PAYMENT

ACCOUNT NUMBER	CLOSING DATE	PAYMENT DUE DATE	MINIMUM PAYMENT
5101 6000 2575 8834	03-27-XX	04-21-XX	$7.00

POSTING DATE	REFERENCE NUMBER	DATE AND DESCRIPTION OF TRANSACTION	$ AMOUNT
03 07	06606220477	PAYMENT – THANK YOU	123.55CR
03 11	07006272091	PAYMENT – THANK YOU	12.47CR
03 16	08553428012	HECHT S - 8	9.37
03 21	05769816532	BRADLEE	46.32

BALANCE PRIOR TO 02-01-XX   BALANCE PRIOR TO 07-01-XX

SUMMARY OF TRANSACTIONS	PREVIOUS BALANCE	− PAYMENTS AND CREDITS	+ PURCHASES AND ADJUSTMENTS	+ CASH ADVANCES	+ FINANCE CHARGE	= NEW BALANCE
BEFORE 03-01-XX	$.00	$.00	$.00	$.00	$.00	$.00
AFTER 02-27-XX	$225.95	$136.02	$55.69	$.00	$2.92	$148.54
TOTAL	$225.95	$136.02	$55.69	$.00	$2.92	$148.54

FINANCE CHARGE SCHEDULE

RANGE OF BALANCES	PERIODIC RATE	ANNUAL PERCENTAGE RATE	BALANCE SUBJECT TO FINANCE CHARGE	METHOD OF CALCULATION OF BALANCE SUBJECT TO FINANCE CHARGE
	BALANCE PRIOR TO 03-01-			SEE REVERSE SIDE
ENTIRE BALANCE	BALANCE AFTER TO 03-01- 1.63% *	19.60% **	$.00	SEE REVERSE SIDE METHOD E

*PERIODIC RATE MAY VARY.

MINIMUM PAYMENT DUE	
PAST DUE AMOUNT	$.00
REVOLVING CREDIT MINIMUM	$.00
MINIMUM PAYMENT	$.00

**RATE NEXT MONTH'S STATEMENT 19.60%

PAGE 1 OF 1

TO AVOID ADDITIONAL FINANCE CHARGE PAY NEW BALANCE BY PAYMENT DUE DATE

YOU MAY CALL THIS NUMBER FOR INFORMATION OR TO REPORT LOSS OR THEFT HOWEVER, BILLING RIGHTS ARE PRESERVED ONLY BY WRITTEN INQUIRIES

806-555-0163

FORWARD BILLING INQUIRIES TO:
PLAINS NATIONAL BANK
PO BOX 271
LUBBOCK TEXAS   79408

Critical Thinking

1. What was the previous balance (amount owed last month)?

   _____

2. What amount was paid last month?

   _____

3. How much was the unpaid balance last month?

   _____

4. What is the total of the new charges?

   _____

5. What is the finance charge?

   _____

6. What is the new balance?

   _____

7. What is the minimum payment that can be made on the new balance?

   _____

8. What is the annual percentage rate of finance charges?

   _____

9. When is the next payment due?

   _____

10. What is the closing date of the statement (the last day bills can be added to the statement)?

    _____

11. What telephone number can you call if you lose your credit card?

    _____

CHAPTER 14 Managing Your Money

ACTIVITY 5   *Being a Consumer*

for use with Lesson 14.2

Your Goal: Give some advice on how to be a good consumer.

What to Do: You are an advice columnist for *Consumer Wise* magazine.
One day you receive the following letter from a reader. In the space that
follows, write the response you would print in your column.

The Letter

```
Dear Consumer Wise:

My friend reads this magazine, and I'm hoping
that he'll read your answer to this letter.

The problem is that my friend doesn't know
how to shop or manage money. He spends money
on anything without even thinking. What
happens? He's never satisfied with what he
buys. I get tired of hearing him complain
about what bad things he buys. Please give
him some advice about how to shop. I think
it's better coming from you than from me.

Sincerely,
Tired of Complaints
```

Your Response

_____

_____

_____

_____

_____

_____

Continued on next page

Critical Thinking

1. In one sentence, state the main problem in the letter from "Tired of Complaints."

_____

_____

_____

_____

_____

_____

_____

_____

_____

2. What other problems might teenagers have in being consumers? List at least three problems teenagers might face as consumers.

_____

_____

_____

_____

_____

_____

_____

_____

_____

_____

_____

_____

CHAPTER 15 Living a Balanced Life

ACTIVITY 1 *Get Your Priorities Straight*
for use with Lesson 15.1

Your Goal: Practice prioritizing your tasks.

What to Do: Read the list of things that Henry has to do. Put them in order of importance. Then practice prioritizing your own tasks.

Henry's Tasks

Henry is a senior in high school. He has many jobs to do this weekend. He is worried that he may not be able to finish all of them.

Here are his tasks for the weekend:
1. Order flowers for prom on Saturday night.
2. Pick up flowers.
3. Mow lawn.
4. Feed the dog.
5. Walk the dog.
6. Write a three-page paper that is due on Monday during period four.
7. Find a current event in the newspaper for history class—due on Thursday.
8. Write letter to Grandma Choi.
9. Send graduation announcements.

Prioritize the Tasks

Write Henry's tasks below in order of importance:

_____

_____

_____

_____

_____

_____

_____

_____

Continued on next page

Now make a list of tasks that YOU must complete in the next week, including schoolwork.

My Tasks

_____

_____

_____

My Tasks in Priority Order

_____

_____

_____

Critical Thinking

1. Did you notice that some tasks that Henry had to do were top priority because of a time deadline? List below the tasks that could not be postponed:

Task:_____   Deadline:_____

Task:_____   Deadline:_____

Task:_____   Deadline:_____

Task:_____   Deadline:_____

Task:_____   Deadline:_____

Task:_____   Deadline:_____

Task:_____   Deadline:_____

2. Do you have any tasks with a time deadline? Which ones? What will happen if you do not complete those tasks?

Task:_____   Time Deadline:_____

What will happen if I don't complete it: _____

Task:_____   Time Deadline:_____

What will happen if I don't complete it: _____

Task:_____   Time Deadline:_____

What will happen if I don't complete it: _____

3. Have you made time for fun and entertainment? What kind of entertainment have you scheduled? List those activities below.

_____

_____

CHAPTER 15 Living a Balanced Life

ACTIVITY 2 *Time-Management Tips*

for use with Lesson 15.1

Your Goal: Learn how to use time-management techniques in your daily life.

What to Do: After looking over the following list of time-management tips, read about a day in the lives of Fred and Frieda, the frazzled twins. Put the letter of the appropriate tip in the blank space at the end of each paragraph. Hint: More than one time-management tip can be used to solve the same problem.

A. Making a "To-Do List": Make a list as a reminder of tasks to complete.
B. Breaking big projects into small steps: Break a big project into smaller manageable tasks.
C. Setting a schedule: Make a list showing when things must be completed.
D. Making a timeline: Show the order of events for a big project on a timeline.

A Day in the Life of Frazzled Fred and Frieda

1. Fred wakes up at 8 A.M. He's late because he stayed up until 1 A.M. to finish his term paper for first period. Now he might be late to class. Fred always waits until the last minute to do everything. **Tip** _____

2. Frieda wakes up thinking about school. "Did I have homework to do? I don't think so," she mutters to herself. **Tip** _____

3. Fred and Frieda catch the bus at 8:30. They just make it to the bus because Fred remembers at the last minute that he has to feed the fish before school. **Tip** _____

4. Frieda gets to first period and then realizes she did have homework. The teacher gives her a zero for the day. **Tip** _____

5. During homeroom, Frieda gets a summons from her guidance counselor. He asks why she has not turned in her class request sheet for next year's classes. Now she won't get the classes she wants. **Tip** _____

6. Fred receives a notice saying that he owes three library books. He starts thinking about where those books might be. **Tip** _____

Continued on next page

7. Frieda feels overwhelmed in drama class. She thinks she will never learn all of her lines for the school play.

Tip _____

8. After school, Fred calls an employer about a part-time job, but he's too late. The job was filled two weeks ago.

Tip _____

Critical Thinking

What suggestions would you have for Fred and Frieda, the frazzled twins?

_____

_____

_____

_____

_____

_____

_____

_____

_____

_____

_____

_____

_____

_____

_____

_____

_____

_____

_____

CHAPTER 15 Living a Balanced Life

ACTIVITY 3 *Community Concerns*

for use with Lesson 15.2

Your Goal: Learn about what is important to the members of your community.

What to Do: Get a copy of your local newspaper. Find out what is happening in your neighborhood. Then answer the following questions:

Read About Your Community

1. How many articles can you find in your local newspaper about the schools in your area?

_____

List the titles and briefly describe the contents of the articles:

_____

_____

_____

_____

2. How many articles can you find about crime? _____

List the titles and briefly describe the contents of the articles:

_____

_____

_____

3. How many articles are about local people? _____

List the titles and briefly describe the contents of the articles:

_____

_____

_____

Continued on next page

4. How many articles are about politics or community disputes? _____

List the titles and briefly describe the contents of the articles:

_____

_____

_____

_____

Exercise Leadership

Write a letter to the editor of your newspaper in response to one of the articles. For example, there might be an article about your school football team. Let the editor know your views on the article. Who knows? Your letter may be printed in the next issue.

My letter to the editor:

_____

_____

_____

_____

_____

_____

_____

_____

_____

Critical Thinking

1. What issues seem to be important in your community? What did you learn about your community and the concerns of the people?

_____

_____

2. Did you see any opportunities to volunteer or help out? If so, where would you call to find out about the opportunities?

_____

_____

_____

CHAPTER **15** Living a Balanced Life

ACTIVITY 4   *Good Citizenship Skills*
for use with Lesson 15.2

Your Goal: Find examples of citizenship skills.

What to Do: Below are listed four important citizenship skills. Explain the citizenship skills to three people in your school, community, or personal life. Then ask them to give you an example of each one.

Citizenship Skills

Respecting Others: Treat members of your community as you would like to be treated.
Caring for What You Share: Take good care of shared property such as parks, libraries, and schools.
Staying Informed: Learn about issues and events in your community.
Making Your Voice Heard: Make your voice heard by such methods as voting or petitioning.

Interview #1

Person interviewed _____
Examples suggested:
Example of Respecting Others _____

_____

Example of Caring for What You Share _____

_____

Example of Staying Informed _____

_____

Example of Making Your Voice Heard _____

_____

Interview #2

Person interviewed _____
Examples suggested:
Example of Respecting Others _____

_____

Continued on next page

Example of Caring for What You Share _____

_____

Example of Staying Informed _____

_____

Example of Making Your Voice Heard _____

_____

Interview #3

Person interviewed _____

Examples suggested:

Example of Respecting Others _____

_____

Example of Caring for What You Share _____

_____

Example of Staying Informed _____

_____

Example of Making Your Voice Heard _____

_____

Critical Thinking

List below three specific things you could do today to practice your citizenship skills.

_____

_____

_____

_____

_____

_____

_____

_____

_____

CHAPTER 15 Living a Balanced Life

ACTIVITY 5 *Taking an Active Role in Your Community*

for use with Lesson 15.2

Your Goal: Learn to do something about school or community problems.

What to Do: Make a list of the things that need to be changed or improved in your school or community. Then write a petition to have something changed. A petition is a formal written request for something.

See how many signatures you can get on your petition. You may even submit your petition to the authorities.

What Can Be Improved in My School

_____

_____

_____

_____

_____

_____

What Can Be Improved in My Community

_____

_____

_____

_____

_____

_____

Continued on next page

Choose one of the problems from your lists on the previous page and write your petition for change.

To: _____

Request for change: _____

_____

_____

_____

_____

The following people support this petition:

Print Full Name   Signature

_____   _____

_____   _____

_____   _____

_____   _____

_____   _____

Critical Thinking

1. How did people respond to your request to sign your petition? Did they agree or disagree with your proposal or complaint?

_____

_____

_____

2. In what other ways could you serve your community? List at least three forms of community service you could perform.

_____

_____

_____

CHAPTER 16 Looking Beyond Today

Moving to a New Neighborhood

for use with Lesson 16.1

Your Goal: Teach young children how to face change in their lives.

What to Do: Write a story for young children about a child who is faced with moving to a new neighborhood. In your story, use the following suggested ways to cope with change.

Ways to Cope with Change

Plan ahead: Prepare for change by finding out all you can about what might happen.

Share your feelings: Talk to friends, family members, or other trusted people about the change.

Find something positive about the change: Look at what you can learn from the experience.

Learn to be supportive: Learn to support others when they are having a hard time.

Write Your Story

_____

_____

_____

_____

_____

_____

_____

_____

_____

_____

_____

_____

_____

_____

Continued on next page

Analyze the Story

1. What changes did the child face?

_____

_____

_____

2. What pictures could you use to illustrate your story?

_____

_____

_____

3. Would your story help a young child adjust to the changes? How would it help?

_____

_____

_____

Critical Thinking

1. Has reading a story or seeing a movie about a problem ever helped you? How?

_____

_____

_____

_____

2. If you had to move to a new neighborhood, which of the four ways to cope with change would help you the most? Why?

_____

_____

_____

_____

CHAPTER 16 Looking Beyond Today

ACTIVITY 2   *The Effects of Change*

for use with Lesson 16.1

Your Goal: Examine the effects of change in a person's life.

What to Do: Have some fun. Think about your favorite people. Imagine what they would do when faced with a sudden change in life.

Hint: Some of the possible changes could be: getting married, getting fired, moving, starting a new job, going to college, having a child, getting divorced, meeting a new stepparent.

Person #1

Name of person: _____

Description of person: _____

What change do you imagine would happen?

_____

_____

_____

What would that person's reaction be?

_____

_____

_____

Person #2

Name of person: _____

Description of person: _____

What change do you imagine would happen?

_____

_____

_____

Continued on next page

What would that person's reaction be?

_____

_____

_____

Person #3

Name of person: _____

Description of person: _____

What change do you imagine would happen?

_____

_____

_____

What would that person's reaction be?

_____

_____

_____

Critical Thinking

Have you faced any changes lately? What were the changes and how did you react?

Change _____

How I reacted _____

_____

Change _____

How I reacted _____

_____

Change _____

How I reacted _____

_____

Change _____

How I reacted _____

_____

CHAPTER 16 Looking Beyond Today

File in your Career Resource File.

ACTIVITY 3   *Be a Lifelong Learner*

for use with Lesson 16.2

Your Goal: Keep a record of all of the new things you learn in one week.

What to Do: Keep a record of everything you learn for one week.

In school:

Monday _____

Tuesday _____

Wednesday _____

Thursday _____

Friday _____

Saturday _____

Sunday _____

On my job or volunteer work:

Monday _____

Tuesday _____

Wednesday _____

Thursday _____

Friday _____

Saturday _____

Sunday _____

In my leisure time:

Monday _____

Tuesday _____

Wednesday _____

Thursday _____

Friday _____

Saturday _____

Sunday _____

Other:

Monday _____

Tuesday _____

Wednesday _____

Thursday _____

Friday _____

Saturday _____

Sunday _____

Critical Thinking

What specific things could you do to learn even more each day?

_____

_____

_____

CHAPTER 16 Looking Beyond Today

File in
your Career
Resource File.

ACTIVITY 4 *A Picture of the Future*

for use with Lesson 16.2

Your Goal: Look at what the future may bring.

What to Do: Create a word picture. Choose words from newspapers and magazines that give a vision of the world in the future. Create a collage using the words. Then answer the questions that follow.

Critical Thinking

1. What did you learn from creating your word picture? List three things you learned.

_____

_____

_____

_____

2. What responsibilities do you have now? List three.

_____

_____

_____

_____

3. What responsibilities do you think you will have in the future? List three.

_____

_____

_____

_____

4. What steps can you take to prepare for the future?

_____

_____

_____

_____

_____

CHAPTER 16 Looking Beyond Today

ACTIVITY 5 *An Apartment of Your Own*

for use with Lesson 16.2

Your Goal: Learn how much it would cost to move into your own apartment.

What to Do: Use the "Apartments for Rent" section of the classified advertisements to do research for this project. Pretend that you are going to move into an apartment on your own. How much would it cost—just to move in?

Average Rent

Unfurnished 1 bedroom _____

Unfurnished 2 bedroom _____

Average Security deposit (You will have to call the apartment manager to get this information)

Unfurnished 1 bedroom _____

Unfurnished 2 bedroom _____

Critical Thinking

1. What do you think now about moving into your own apartment? How much money would you need to make on your job in order to pay for your rent?

_____

_____

_____

_____

_____

2. What other costs do you think you would have? List them below. Will you need furniture, telephone service, cable hookup?

_____

_____

_____

_____

_____

Continued on next page

Chapter 16 • Exploring Careers 183

3. What other expenses will you have after you move in? Will you have to pay for your own food and clothes, laundry services, etc.? What about entertainment? List below some of the other expenses you will have when you live on your own.

_____

_____

_____

_____

_____

4. Would you like to have a roommate to share the costs? Why or why not?

_____

_____

_____

_____

_____

_____